# Freedom Song

## Young Voices and the Struggle for Civil Rights

## Mary C. Turck

CHICAGO
REVIEW
PRESS

**Library of Congress Cataloging-in-Publication Data**
Turck, Mary.
    Freedom song : young voices and the struggle for civil rights / Mary C. Turck.
        p. cm.
    Includes bibliographical references and index.
    ISBN 978-1-55652-773-9

1. African Americans—Civil rights—History—20th century—Juvenile literature. 2. Civil rights movements—United States—History—20th century—Juvenile literature. 3. Youth—United States—Political activity—History—20th century—Juvenile literature. 4. African Americans—Music—Political aspects—History—20th century—Juvenile literature. 5. Music—Political aspects—United States—History—20th century—Juvenile literature. 6. Singing—Political aspects—United States—History—20th century—Juvenile literature. 7. Choirs (Music)—Political aspects—United States—History—20th century—Juvenile literature. 8. Church music—Political aspects—United States—History—20th century—Juvenile literature. 9. Chicago Children's Choir—History—Juvenile literature. 10. Freedom Singers—History—Juvenile literature. I. Title.

E185.61.T845 2009

323.0973—dc22

2008029673

Cover and interior design: Scott Rattray
Cover photographs: (left) © J. Philips; (center) © Bob Adelman; (right) © 2008 Chicago Children's Choir
Page 12 photograph: Peeter Viisimaa/iStockphoto

Published by Chicago Review Press, Incorporated
814 North Franklin Street
Chicago, Illinois 60610
ISBN 978-1-55652-773-9
Printed in the United States of America
5 4 3 2 1

*To the people of the civil rights movement, both the leaders and those whose names never made it into a single history book*

*To the people who work for justice today, persevering despite defeat and disappointment*

*To the people whose music supports and uplifts us along the way, and especially to St. Dominic's gospel choir, who introduced me to gospel music and convinced me to open my mouth and sing*

# Contents

# Acknowledgments

First, I owe a deep debt of gratitude to Geof Stone, chair of the board of the Chicago Children's Choir (CCC). Without his persistence and his passion for the CCC and the civil rights movement, this book would never have been written. Geof's involvement, from the book proposal through the first editing stage, helped to shape and improve the book.

Many thanks also to the CCC singers and staff, who welcomed my family and me, both in Chicago and on the Freedom Tour. Your voices appear throughout the book, so I will not try to name individuals here—except for Davin Peelle, the behind-the-scenes contact, who has been an invaluable liaison and problem solver. Thanks also to the CCC alums who shared their stories.

Mollie Spector Stone, associate conductor of the CCC, has a unique role in both the choir and this book. She is an alum of the choir who returned as a professional musician, whose passion for music is matched by her passion for justice. Her professional work in South Africa was inspired by her teenage travel there on a CCC concert tour. I am deeply grateful to her for sharing her knowledge of African and South African music.

Hollis Watkins and Chuck McDew shared generously of their time, stories, and memories. I have known Chuck for years but met Hollis only because of this book. They are both true American heroes. I wish that every person who reads this book could have the opportunity to meet them, to hear them speak, and to thank them for the blood, sweat, and tears they have given to make a better country and a better world for generations to come.

Thanks also to Jackie Byrd Martin in McComb, to Dr. Alferdteen Harrison and Angela Stewart at Jackson State University, and to Robert Williams, David Baker, and Joe West in Birmingham for sharing their stories of the past and present.

Thanks to my publisher and editor, Cynthia Sherry of Chicago Review Press, who has worked with me to make this book much better than it would have been without her guidance and care.

Finally, thanks to my family—Ron, Molly, and Macy Salzberger—for traveling on the Freedom Tour and for putting up with the demands of the book-writing process. Thanks also to my parents, Howard and Millie Turck, who long ago instilled in me a passion for justice and for the civil rights movement.

As every author says and knows, the contributions of many people went into making this book, but any errors that have crept in are entirely my own.

# THE MOVEMENT, THE MUSIC, AND THE CHICAGO CHILDREN'S CHOIR

Imagine yourself back in the 1950s. A loaf of bread cost 14 cents. Color television was new and exciting. Barbie dolls appeared for the first time. Popular fads included hula hoops, coonskin caps, and Silly Putty. Elvis Presley recorded hit songs, including "Heartbreak Hotel" and "Hound Dog." Dwight D. Eisenhower was president. The United States fought a war in Korea that ended in 1953. Most people in the United States were afraid of Russia and its communist government. (In theory, the communist system held that the government should directly control all industry and share its economic benefits equally with all people, but in practice the Russian government was repressive toward its own citizens and hostile to the United States.)

Many people feared change of any kind, but change of all kinds was happening. In the South, *segregation* was the law. Segregation laws separated black and white people. In 1954, the U.S. Supreme Court said that school segregation, the separation of people because of race or skin color, violated the U.S. Constitution.

A movement for civil rights was growing. The civil rights movement found its greatest challenges and opportunities in the segregated southern United States. From water fountains to movie theaters, laws ordered separation

This drinking fountain shows the separation of black and white people in the South before the civil rights movement. Black people and white people were not even allowed to drink from the same fountains. *John Vachon, 1938, courtesy of the Library of Congress*

women and the NAACP began to organize. They called for mass protest meetings. By December 5, black residents of Montgomery had agreed to *boycott* the bus system—meaning that they would refuse to ride the city's buses at all until the unfair treatment ended.

The leaders of the bus boycott included many local ministers, including the Reverend Martin Luther King Jr., and the campaign started with meetings in the churches. People at the meetings sang as a way of praying. They sang to express their deepest feelings. In the songs, they connected with one another. Their passion and commitment to the movement and to one another grew through the singing. And just about one year after the boycott began, they won—segregation on Montgomery buses ended.

of black people and white people. Signs reserved the best places for "whites only." Many restaurants would not serve black people at all.

On December 1, 1955, Rosa Parks was arrested in Montgomery, Alabama. She was charged with the crime of refusing to give up her seat on a bus to a white man. Rosa Parks worked as a seamstress. She was also a member of the National Association for the Advancement of Colored People (NAACP), a civil rights organization. Rosa Parks was ready to fight back. Immediately, local black university

Back in 1956, as the bus boycott was nearing victory in Alabama, a new minister came to the First Unitarian Church in Chicago. His name was Chris Moore. He was young and energetic. He was a musician. And he was also filled with the spirit of the civil rights movement. He believed deeply in the equality of all people and in the need to work for justice.

Chris Moore started a children's choir.

Chicago is a northern city, so it did not have strict segregation laws like those in the South. But Moore

COLORED

understood that this did not mean the city was integrated. Far from it! Segregation in the South was enforced by law. Segregation in the North was enforced by simple racism.

In Chicago, black people and white people lived in different neighborhoods. Real estate agents would not sell homes in "white neighborhoods" to black families. If a black family managed to buy a home in a white neighborhood, they faced violence. They might be shunned by their neighbors or even attacked on the street. Their home could be vandalized, or worse. Because housing was segregated, schools were segregated too. Schools in black neighborhoods were for black children. Schools in white neighborhoods were for white children.

Chris Moore, however, believed in *integration*—in bringing people of different races together instead of separating them. His mother had been involved in Unitarian service work on Navajo reservations and in Nigeria. At First Unitarian, Moore found a church with the same commitment. Back in 1948, First Unitarian had passed a resolution "to invite our friends of other races and colors who are interested in Unitarianism to join our church."

The First Unitarian Church was in Chicago's Hyde Park neighborhood. Hyde Park is located in the part of Chicago called the South Side. The University of Chicago is in Hyde Park. Many professors and students live there. Hyde Park is an integrated neighborhood. It is a well-to-do neighborhood. Poorer neighborhoods surround Hyde Park—Woodlawn, Kenwood, Washington

Park, Englewood, and Oakland. These neighborhoods are mostly black. That is the way Chicago looked in 1956. That is still largely the way it looks today.

At first, Moore's choir was made up of children from the First Unitarian Church, but he moved quickly to include other children, especially black children from economically poor neighborhoods. As director, Moore insisted on two things: The choir would help children to become excellent singers, never compromising on quality. And it would include children of all races and economic backgrounds on an equal level, never compromising on justice. The choir that Chris Moore started grew into the Chicago Children's Choir.

Rob Eller-Isaacs joined the choir when he was seven years old. As an adult, he recalled the experience:

> Here we were, middle-class kids from the chronically overeducated Hyde Park, getting to know and become friends with kids who lived in the projects. Kids from all over the city. Not out of *noblesse oblige* [a feeling that the privileged are obligated to help the less fortunate], but out of a common commitment to musical excellence.

In 1975, Moore wrote about his life for the 25th reunion of classmates from Harvard University:

> I have been deeply concerned about this country and the world in which we live. My way of attempting to help change it has been working with children and youth in

Today the Chicago Children's Choir provides music programs to dozens of Chicago elementary schools, and offers eight after-school neighborhood choirs. The Hyde Park neighborhood choir is pictured here. *Andrea Bechert, courtesy of the Chicago Children's Choir*

and through music to assist them to a deeper understanding of the whole process of building and maintaining a culture that nourishes and ministers to its people. . . . And when that process includes the . . . fortunate side by side with street kids and those of every imaginable background and circumstance, and nothing is of importance but the persons themselves and what they are about together, then I begin to feel that there may be some substance to that American Dream of the open society that we have so often preferred to mouth rather than to accept to live.

Moore died in 1987, but the Chicago Children's Choir continues. So does its commitment to racial equality and justice.

From the first dozen children, the Chicago Children's Choir has grown to include thousands of children each year. Today, there are almost 3,000 children involved in the choir. Some sing in school choirs in the dozens of Chicago-area schools served by the choir. Others sing in CCC's neighborhood choirs in Hyde Park, Albany Park, Beverly, Garfield Park, Humboldt Park, Lincoln Park, Pilsen/Little Village, and Rogers Park. Each year about 100 talented singers participate in the Concert Choir. This choir travels and sings on national and international tours. In recent years, the Chicago Children's Choir has performed throughout the world, from South Africa to Scotland, from the Czech Republic to Italy, from Russia to Japan.

Under artistic director Josephine Lee, the CCC performs regularly with the Chicago Symphony Orchestra, the Joffrey Ballet, and the Lyric Opera of Chicago. In recent years, it has performed at Carnegie Hall in New York City, Constitution Hall in Washington, D.C., and the Democratic National Convention.

The choir has performed for President Bill Clinton, South African president Nelson Mandela, the Dalai Lama, Archbishop Desmond Tutu, and Queen Noor of Jordan. Over the years the children have performed with or for such varied and distinguished artists as Luciano Pavarotti, Sir Georg Solti, Harry Belafonte, Quincy Jones, Willie Pickens, Gwendolyn Brooks, Roberta Flack, Samuel Ramey, Bobby McFerrin, and Ladysmith Black Mambazo. In 2006, the CCC's production of *Sita Ram*, an original musical rendering of the *Ramayana*, the Indian creation epic, was nominated for three Jefferson Awards (the Chicago version of the Tony Awards given to theatrical productions in New York City).

Celebrating its 50th anniversary year, the CCC looked for a way to mark its historic commitment to civil rights. The CCC wanted to tell the story of the civil rights movement to new generations. In the summer of 2007, as part of its anniversary celebration, the CCC sent a group of its most talented singers on an extended tour of the American South. They retraced the steps of the heroes and martyrs of the civil rights movement. They cried in the Slavery Museum, reenacting the journey from Africa. They sang in Birmingham, in a church that had been bombed in 1963, standing in the place where Reverend Martin Luther King Jr. had preached. They walked over Selma's Edmund Pettus Bridge, following the footsteps of people who had been bloodied and beaten to the ground simply because they wanted the rights guaranteed by the U.S. Constitution. They sang at the Lorraine Hotel in Memphis, beneath the balcony where Dr. King was assassinated in 1968. The CCC's Freedom Tour was

the inspiration for *Freedom Song*. Many of the songs they sang on the Freedom Tour are included in the CD at the back of this book. Throughout the book, "Voices of the Choir" sidebars offer the reflections of choir members.

This book tells the story of the civil rights movement through the freedom songs that strengthened its soul and served as its voice. *Freedom Song* looks back on 50 years of the CCC—and beyond, to the roots of the civil rights movement. Young people have been leaders and dreamers and martyrs in the movement. This book tells the stories of the music they brought to the movement, the music that accompanied and inspired the struggle through the years. Along the way, *Freedom Song* also tells stories of young people whose lives and commitment to justice were enriched by their participation in the Chicago Children's Choir. (For more on the CCC, see www.ccchoir.org)

The civil rights movement continues today, North and South, East and West. Today it takes many different forms—civil rights for people of color, for gay people, for immigrants, for students, for people around the globe. Music weaves through the movement, expressing its soul and giving hope and strength to those who made it happen "back then," and to those who still march and pray and sing and work for freedom and justice. Moving from slavery days to the 21st century, *Freedom Song* tells the story of music and the movement for freedom and equality and justice.

Cece Hill sang in the Chicago Children's Choir for 10 years, from third grade through her high school graduation in 1993. Today she works for the choir as program manager. She describes how the choir works:

"When Christopher Moore started the choir, he figured that if he brought every race and nationality together, it would prove that segregation is not the way. We can all get along. We can all get along through music. We took that and ran with it over the years. We use different styles of music, we travel all over the world, we use that as our vehicle to get around. When you say 'civil rights,' people get it. We stand for it. We represent it to the world.

"When kids come to audition, they are very tense or nervous. When they walk into this room and they see every nationality, every religion, everything in this one room, it's like, 'Whoa—what is this?' All of these stereotypes that are embedded in everyone's mind, they're all checked at the door. They're not represented at all when they come to the choir."

Cece Hill with two young choir members on tour. *Mary C. Turck*

**"We can all get along. We can all get along through music."**

# Freedom Song

## Chapter 1

Sunday of Song

# You are important to me, I need you to survive

During the early years of the civil rights movement, black churches were much more than religious buildings. Because of segregation, they also served their communities as cultural and political centers. Churches were where civil rights activists would come together to plan their demonstrations. In Birmingham, Alabama, these meetings took place every Monday night, moving from church to church. If too many meetings were held in one church, it would become known as the "civil rights church." It would become a target for racists, who might bomb or burn it. By moving around, people hoped to keep their churches safe.

On a September Sunday in 1963, the basement of the 16th Street Baptist Church in Birmingham echoed with chatter and laughter. Teenagers combed their hair and checked themselves in the mirrors. That Sunday, on Youth Day, they would lead the services. They were ready to stand in front of everyone, ready to lead, ready for life.

And then life ended. A bomb blast shook the church, tumbled the walls, and killed four young girls. Their church was bombed, their lives were ended, by racists attacking black people and the civil rights movement.

Nearly 45 years later, another group of young people assembled in the same church basement. Once again, young people combed their hair and checked themselves in the mirrors. On the first day of their Freedom Tour, the Chicago Children's Choir got ready to sing in the 16th Street Baptist Church.

At this concert, the pews of the church were filled with a mostly black audience. The people listening to the choir carried the history of their church in their hearts. Many had lived through the civil rights movement. Others had parents and grandparents who had been in the movement.

They listened as the choir sang "Murder on the Road in Alabama" and cried "Deep within the sovereign state of Alabama / There's a poison pit of hate." They listened to "Strange Fruit," the song made famous by Billie Holiday that mourned murdered black men hanging from southern trees. "Birmingham Sunday," a ballad of grief,

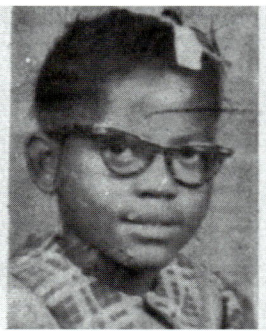

Today the four young girls who died in the Birmingham church bombing are commemorated in a memorial that bears their photos. *From left*, Denise McNair, 11, Carole Robertson, 14, Addie Mae Collins, 14, and Cynthia Wesley, 14, are shown in these 1963 photos. *Associated Press*

ence rose, singing with the Chicago teens, "I need you. You need me. . . . You are important to me. . . . I love you, I need you to survive." They continued, closing the powerful afternoon arm in arm, singing "We Shall Overcome." In an electric moment, voices and hearts connected across the years, across the generations.

recalled the events of that 1963 Sunday when four schoolgirls were killed and one maimed. (All of these songs are on the Chicago Children's Choir CD that accompanies this book, *Songs on the Road to Freedom*.)

The songs struck home. Sixteenth Street Baptist will forever be the church of four young girls killed by a Sunday morning bomb blast. In this very church, Dr. Martin Luther King Jr. preached. In this very church, Monday night meetings of civil rights activists filled the air with song. Across the street, in the park, police set dogs on civil rights demonstrators, and powerful fire hoses knocked the demonstrators over like bowling pins.

On the July afternoon in 2007, music flowed through the 16th Street Baptist Church. The music wove a powerful connection between singers and audience, between past and present. As people listened, their hands reached up in the air, swaying in time to the songs. Then the audi-

## Then and Now: McComb, Mississippi

The U.S. civil rights movement of the 1950s and 1960s won huge victories. Despite those victories, racism continues. McComb, Mississippi, shows both the victories of the movement and the continuing struggle for civil rights.

In 1961, a teenager named Jackie Byrd knelt on the steps of the McComb courthouse. Young people in McComb had seized the civil rights movement as their own. The protests in McComb included attempts to integrate the public library, the Woolworth's lunch counter, and the Greyhound bus station. The movement in McComb included a *Freedom School* (in 1961 and again in 1964), and voter registration attempts at the nearby county seat of Magnolia. Freedom Schools taught adults to read and write, and to understand their rights under the Constitution.

The students who protested against segregation and prayed at the courthouse were jailed. More than 100 students were sent to jail. Then they were expelled from their high school for protesting. Jackie Byrd was among those who were expelled. They went to a black junior college in Jackson, Mississippi, for the rest of the school year.

Today Jackie Byrd Martin sits at a desk inside the same courthouse. She is the city's personnel director. The window of her office overlooks the steps where she and other young protesters prayed and were arrested over 45 years ago. The "whites only" sign is long gone from the water fountain across the hall. McComb's first black mayor was inaugurated in 2007. He held the ceremony on the courthouse steps.

McComb's population, about 12,000 in 1961, has grown little over the decades. The 2000 census showed 13,337 residents, about 58 percent of whom are black. Legal segregation has ended. That is a victory of the civil

The Chicago Children's Choir sang in the historic 16th Street Baptist Church, which was deeply involved in the civil rights movement in Birmingham. The church was bombed in 1963, killing four young girls. *Mary C. Turck*

rights movement. Today black people hold positions in city government. That is a victory of the civil rights movement. McComb has come a long way since 1961.

But not everything has changed. In 2007, the schools in McComb and in nearby South Pike are at least 80 percent black. The schools in nearby North Pike are 80 percent white. A local Christian school is virtually all white.

## I Need You to Survive

*I need you, you need me*
*We're all a part of God's body . . .*
*You are important to me, I need you to survive . . .*
*I love you, I need you to survive . . .*

This gospel song has become a signature for the Chicago Children's Choir. They perform it often, and it has become part of their identity. The CCC is more than a singing group. For many people it is family and love and support. Robert Raymond, 17, describes the meaning that the song has for him:

"This song does the best job out of all describing the choir. When I try and think about my life if I hadn't joined choir, it is impossible because it has made me so much of who I am. I have become worldly conscious and problem-questioning, and the relationships that I have made here are stronger than any others. This song illustrates our unity while we sing in unison and then shows our differences that make the choir so rich when it splits off into different parts. I really do need my family—the members of the choir past and present—to survive. The relationships will not die with distance because who I am depends on my family to live on."

(To hear the Chicago Children's Choir sing this song, visit www.rhapsody.com/chicagochildrenschoir/openupyourheart/ineedyoutosurvive.)

**"When I try and think about my life if I hadn't joined choir, it is impossible because it has made me so much of who I am."**

As of this writing, McComb's tourist brochures still do not mention 1961 or the students or the civil rights movement. The pictures on the courthouse walls show only white folks and historical events from before the 1960s. The official City of McComb Web site (www.mccomb-ms.com) does not mention the civil rights movement. The unofficial McComb Web site (www.mccombms.com) includes a lengthy history page that describes railroads, oil, camellias, and azaleas—but not the civil rights movement.

Another site, McComb Legacies (www.mccomblega cies.org), tells the civil rights story of McComb. This site describes the city as "one of the main battlegrounds in the struggle for civil rights in the United States." McComb Legacies features oral histories from the civil rights era. The McComb Legacies Web site links to the official City of McComb site, but the official site does not link back. The contrasting sites show both the strength of the civil rights legacy and the continuing division between the races in the 21st century.

Jackie Byrd Martin is proud of McComb's civil rights legacy. She hands out brochures for a civil rights driving tour of McComb. She is working with McComb schools to create a model curriculum about the civil rights era. She hopes that curriculum will become a model for the entire state.

Her success shows the progress that McComb has made since the 1960s. The continuing school segregation shows how far the city still has to go. McComb is not so different from other cities, North and South. Success and struggle still live side by side. Quiet heroes like Jackie Byrd Martin continue the movement for freedom, equality, and justice.

## Then and Now: Chicago

In the 1950s, racial segregation in the South was a matter of law. Discrimination against black people was not only allowed but legally required. This is called *de jure* segregation. *De jure* is a Latin phrase meaning "in law." At the time, Chicago, like most northern cities, was also segregated. But in the North segregation was usually not *de jure* but *de facto*—a term meaning "in fact." Under *de facto* segregation, the law did not actually call for racial discrimination, but many other practices kept segregation in place.

For example, in most northern cities, black people could only live in black neighborhoods, not because it was illegal for them to buy houses or rent apartments in white neighborhoods but because no one would sell or rent to them. Some homes were sold with *restrictive covenants* between buyer and seller. A restrictive covenant might say that the person who bought the home could not later sell it to black people. Some restrictive covenants said that the home could not be sold to Jews. In the 1950s, these covenants were enforced by law. Even without restrictive covenants, people discriminated. Real estate agents would only show black people homes in black neighborhoods. If a black family moved into a white neighborhood, they faced the wrath of neighbors.

Black people also faced job discrimination. Some employers would not hire them at all. Others would hire them but pay them less than white workers. Lower wages kept them in poverty. Chicago built housing projects for poor people. The projects were built in black neighborhoods, and crowded with up to 19 floors of apartments. Children played on tiny, tar-topped "tot lots" in between the buildings.

Dr. Martin Luther King Jr. came to Chicago in 1966. People in the civil rights movement had decided to bring the fight to the North. They recognized that discrimination was not just a southern problem. Racism lived in the North as well.

Dr. King's project was called the Chicago Freedom Movement. In the spring of 1966, Chicago Freedom Movement sent "testers" to try to buy houses. The testers were one white couple and one black couple. They were exact matches in income and family size and background. Real estate agents sent the black couple to black neighborhoods. They would not show the black couples homes in white neighborhoods.

Dr. King began to lead protest marches in white Chicago neighborhoods. Marchers were met by screaming mobs. Angry white people threw rocks and bricks and bottles. King received death threats. He said he experienced more hatred in Chicago than he ever did in Mississippi or Alabama.

In July 1966, some 50,000 people attended a civil rights rally at Chicago's Soldier Field. The rally was followed by a march to city hall, where King nailed 14 demands to the door. The demands included open housing and jobs and better schools.

In August, Mayor Richard J. Daley (whose son Richard M. Daley was elected mayor in 1989) agreed to meet with Dr. King's Chicago Freedom Movement. They reached agreement on actions the city would take, but the city did not live up to the agreements. However, in 1968 a national fair housing law was passed that ended restrictive covenants and outlawed discrimination in housing.

Despite this progress, housing segregation continues. A 2006 study showed that 30 percent of all public schools in Chicago were 100 percent African American. Almost half of the schools were 90 percent or more African American. The median income for African American households was only two-thirds of the median for white households. A higher percentage of African Americans were—and still are—among the working poor.

Fear keeps people apart, too. People of different races have little contact with one another. They rarely socialize. They hear stories about other races that are simply untrue. Because they have little contact, they often believe what they hear. People of all races experience this separation.

Both discrimination and the civil rights movement existed in the North as well as the South. This demonstrator is being carried to a police wagon in New York City in 1963. World Telegram & Sun *photo by Dick Demarsico, courtesy of the Library of Congress*

Rachel Andrews was in the Chicago Children's Choir from 1971 to 1981. Later, in college, she studied architecture. Then she changed course. She went back to school to study music. Today she is a mezzo-soprano, singing and teaching music. She reflects on racial divides in Chicago schools, and on her experience in the Chicago Children's Choir:

"I always knew that the magic behind the choir was the mix of classes and mix of races. I went to Kenwood for high school and there was such a racial divide there. In the choir, you never got that. There were people in the choir who wouldn't socialize in the high school, but they would socialize in the choir. I think it was being worried about how they were being perceived. The class structure at Kenwood was awkward. The honors system created an instantaneous segregation that was really unfortunate.

"We were singing music that crossed the lines on both ends. We had white kids singing solos on black gospel songs. We were taught to be all as one.

"We were always doing civil rights songs. [Choir founder and director] Chris Moore was always so politically minded. He was always trying to give a positive sense of the world, to reflect the world in a positive way."

Christopher Moore, founder of the Chicago Children's Choir, sings with the choir. *Courtesy of the Chicago Children's Choir*

**"I always knew that the magic behind the choir was the mix of classes and mix of races."**

# Looking Back, Looking Ahead

Robert Williams, a black Alabaman who was part of the civil rights movement in the 1950s and 1960s, says that "everything has changed—and about 70 percent for the better." In 1969 or 1970, he says, "doors to the real world and corporate America opened for young black people."

For him, the civil rights movement ended in 1969, after the assassinations of Malcolm X, Dr. Martin Luther King Jr., and Robert Kennedy. "We lost too many people at one time," he says. "Vietnam had a lot to do with it, too. There was too much pain, too much struggle, and we didn't want our children to feel that."

The older generation protected their children from the pain and struggle. By doing so, they also lost a vital connection. "We thought our children would feel what we felt about the movement, and they don't," Williams reports, with regret. "They've missed that connection. . . . This is all ancient history for our grandchildren."

Robert Williams brought his grandchildren to a concert on the Freedom Tour. He talked with the Chicago teens in the choir, telling stories of the movement. For him, the civil rights movement will always live. His stories and their songs brought the movement back to the Unitarian Church in Birmingham on a Sunday morning.

Birmingham's Unitarian Church is mostly white. Robert Williams is one of its few black members. (He jokes that his family cannot understand how a good Baptist could become a Unitarian.) This congregation has been committed to civil rights for over 50 years. The church was integrated back in the 1950s. It received bomb threats from time to time. The threats were frequent enough for the church secretary to develop a standard response. She would tell threatening callers that they would have to "stand in line."

David Baker is a white member of the church. He lived in Birmingham in 1961. He remembers when the city closed its parks. It chose to keep everyone out, rather than let black people in. He was active in opposing the closure.

Joe West, another white church member, returned to Birmingham in 1989. He says that today black people can work and live on a better basis than before—even if not on a completely equal basis. "There is still discrimination," he insists. "But there is discrimination throughout the country. Remember, women earn only two-thirds of what men earn. Black people are in the same kind of situation."

The civil rights movement was about justice. Black people were treated unjustly. They suffered discrimination in schools, jobs, housing, and more. The law allowed injustice. Sometimes the law *was* the injustice, ordering segregation and inequality.

The civil rights movement changed laws. The movement won victories. But the struggle for justice and equality continues.

Chapter 2

Rooted in Africa

# Children, run, you got a right
## You got a right to the tree of life

The music of the civil rights movement has many flavors. Some of the old spirituals sung by slaves in the South became part of the civil rights tradition. Jazz musicians composed music for the movement. Other civil rights music came from gospel songs. In the 21st century, some rap musicians contribute songs with messages of justice and equality. But all of these distinctively American musical forms—whether spirituals, gospel music, jazz, blues, soul, rock 'n' roll, rap, or hip-hop—have their roots in Africa.

African rhythms and words and instruments came to North and South America with kidnapped Africans crowded in the bellies of slave ships. In the Americas, African music mixed with music of other places and peoples. After surviving slavery, the music of Africa became part of a rich stew of sound and song and dance.

## The Music of Africa

In Africa, music was part of life. It flowed through daily routine as blood flows through the veins. Songs marked special events, from weddings to a child's first tooth. Warriors sang battle songs. People sang as they cooked or harvested or cared for children. Music did not belong to musicians. Music was not experienced as a performance with performers and audience—everyone sang, everyone danced, everyone made music.

And when they made music, they used many kinds of instruments. One African instrument was the *djembe*, a kind of drum. Another was the banjo. Gourds and sticks and tambourines also had their roots in Africa. *Juba*—using your body to make music—is also part of the African tradition. Singers clap, tap their feet, and slap their thighs to accompany their voices.

African music and European music are similar in many ways—they both use melody, harmony, and rhythm—but some of the rhythms sound quite different. African music is more *polyrhythmic*, which means that it emphasizes combinations of different rhythms. *Syncopation*—stressing a beat that is normally unstressed—is a characteristic African rhythm. Today syncopation is widely used in popular music.

Different areas of Africa have different kinds of music. Because most of the people sold into slavery came from the region of West Africa, African American music basically has West African roots. In West Africa, as in the country of South Africa (see chapter 7), much of the singing is *a cappella*. This means that people sing without instrumental accompaniment. Some West African singing is nasal, and uses shouts and groans and falsetto. A lot of South African music is choral, sung in four-part harmony.

Physical movement is an important part of both West African and South African music. Clapping hands and stamping feet add to music. Dancing is part of some songs. Some movements tell stories.

European vocal music includes folk songs, but places more emphasis on written music. African vocal tradition features much more improvisation. African music comes from oral traditions. Most music is learned orally. People learn songs by singing. In *call-and-response* songs, the leader sings a line, then others either repeat that line or "reply" with a different line.

## From Africa to North America

These African musical traditions began to evolve into African American music when the first African slaves were brought to North America in 1619. Black Africans were kidnapped from their homes, carried to the coast, packed in ships like cargo, carried across the Atlantic

Africans on the deck of the slave ship *Wildfire*, April 30, 1860. *From Harper's Weekly, June 2, 1860, courtesy of the Library of Congress*

Ocean, and sold as slaves to the highest bidders. Millions died during the infamous Middle Passage across the Atlantic. Others died during their first decades in the cruel new world. Millions more survived.

Most of the slaves came from West Africa, an area that today includes the countries of Benin, Burkina Faso, Ivory Coast, Cape Verde, Gambia, Ghana, Guinea, Guinea-Bissau, Liberia, Mali, Mauritania, Niger, Nigeria, Senegal, Sierra Leone, and Togo. During the 17th and 18th centuries, many of these countries did not yet exist. Instead, the people of West Africa were organized in smaller social units. They came from many different ethnic groups. They spoke different languages and sang different songs. They practiced different religions. They sometimes made war on one another. But once they were shipped across the sea, they were all Africans together.

Olaudah Equiano was sold into slavery in West Africa in about 1745. After working for a British naval officer, he gained his freedom in about 1789 and wrote his life story.

As a boy, Equiano was kidnapped and forced into slavery in another community in Africa. This kind of slavery was common. People might become slaves by losing a war or by being captured. They might remain slaves, or they might be adopted into a family and freed. He was not so lucky. He was sold to a British slave trader. Crowded below deck on a ship, the slaves set sail for the Americas.

Equiano wrote of his experience on board the slave ship:

Olaudah Equiano. *From the book cover of The Interesting Narrative of the Life of Olaudah Equiano, or Gustavus Vassa, the African, 1794, Rare Book and Special Collections Division, Library of Congress*

I now saw myself deprived of all chance of returning to my native country, or even the least glimpse of hope of gaining the shore, which I now considered as friendly; and I even wished for my former slavery in preference to my present situation, which was filled with horrors of every kind, still heightened by my ignorance of what I was to undergo. I was not long suffered to indulge my grief; I was soon put down under the decks, and there I received such a salutation in my nostrils as I had never experienced in my life: so that, with the loathsomeness of the stench, and crying together, I became so sick and low that I was not able to eat, nor had I the least desire to taste any thing. I now wished for the last friend, death, to relieve me; but soon, to my grief, two of the white men offered me eatables; and, on my refusing to eat, one of them held me fast by the hands, and laid me across, I think the windlass, and tied my feet, while the other flogged me severely. I had never experienced any thing of this kind before, and although not being used to the water, I naturally feared that element the first time I saw it, yet, nevertheless, could I have got over the nettings, I would have jumped over the side, but I could not; and besides, the crew used to watch us very closely who were not chained down to the decks, lest we should leap into the water; and I have seen some of these poor African prisoners most severely cut, for attempting to do so, and hourly whipped for not eating. This indeed was often the case with myself. In a little time after, amongst the poor chained men, I found some of my own nation, which in a small degree gave ease to my mind. I inquired of these what was to be done with us? They gave me to understand, we were to be carried to these white people's country to work for them. I then was a little revived, and thought, if it were no worse than working, my situation was not so desperate; but still I feared I should be put to death, the white people looked and acted, as I thought, in so savage a manner; for I had never seen among any people such instances of brutal cruelty; and this not only shown towards us blacks, but also to some of the whites themselves.

Some slaves were sold in the North, where they worked in homes and on farms, but most of them were sold in the South. There, slave labor built wealth for slave owners. Slaves labored in the fields, growing tobacco, rice, and indigo.

By the time of the Revolutionary War in 1776, African slaves were a major part of the population of the colonies. The first U.S. census in 1790 showed a total population of 3.9 million. Nineteen percent of the population was counted as black. This included almost 700,000 slaves and about 59,000 free black persons.

Toward the end of the 17th century, cotton arrived in America. Seeds from the East Indies were brought to Virginia. With the invention of the cotton gin in the 1790s, cotton grew in importance. By the mid–19th century, cotton ruled the economy of the South. Some thought it ruled the economy of the world.

The labor of slaves produced the cotton that made the South and, indeed, the entire country wealthy. Slaves cleared fields and planted crops. They chopped cotton, hacking out weeds under a blazing sun. When the fields showed fluffy, white bolls, they picked the cotton. Pickers filled the huge sacks they carried on their backs. They had to work quickly, hands bleeding from the sharp spines on the tips of the cotton bolls. Moving slowly could mean punishment by whipping.

Though the importing of slaves ended in 1808, their numbers continued to grow. The children of slaves were themselves born into slavery. By 1860, the number of African slaves in the South had increased to almost four million. And despite the great hardships they were forced to endure, music continued to live in their hearts. Music vibrated in their bones. They sang the songs and rhythms of Africa. Slave owners were made uneasy by language they could not understand. They tried to forbid African music and songs. Fearing that African drums would pass messages of rebellion, they banned them. The slaves made new music on spoons and pots and washboards. Nothing the slave owners did could stop the music that lived in African people.

In their new country, African slaves continued the tradition of incorporating music into their daily routine. They sang while chopping cotton or picking tobacco.

Sometimes songs set the pace for work or established a common rhythm for people working together. Sometimes music made hard work feel easier or helped the time pass more quickly. One type of work song was a *field holler* (also called a field yell). Field hollers were chanted or yelled more than sung to a melody. Blues music is rooted in field hollers.

# $200 Reward.

RANAWAY from the subscriber, on the night of Thursday, the 30th of Sepember.

# FIVE NEGRO SLAVES,

To-wit: one Negro man, his wife, and three children.

The man is a black negro, full height, very erect, his face a little thin. He is about forty years of age, and calls himself *Washington Reed*, and is known by the name of Washington. He is probably well dressed, possibly takes with him an ivory headed cane, and is of good address. Several of his teeth are gone.

*Mary*, his wife, is about thirty years of age, a bright mulatto woman, and quite stout and strong.

The oldest of the children is a boy, of the name of FIELDING, twelve years of age, a dark mulatto, with heavy eyelids. He probably wore a new cloth cap.

MATILDA, the second child, is a girl, six years of age, rather a dark mulatto, but a bright and smart looking child.

MALCOLM, the youngest, is a boy, four years old, a lighter mulatto than the last, and about equally as bright. He probably also wore a cloth cap. If examined, he will be found to have a swelling at the navel.

Washington and Mary have lived at or near St. Louis, with the subscriber, for about 15 years.

It is supposed that they are making their way to Chicago, and that a white man accompanies them, that they will travel chiefly at night, and most probably in a covered wagon.

A reward of $150 will be paid for their apprehension, so that I can get them, if taken within one hundred miles of St. Louis, and $200 if taken beyond that, and secured so that I can get them, and other reasonable additional charges, if delivered to the subscriber, or to THOMAS ALLEN, Esq., at St. Louis, Mo. The above negroes, for the last few years, have been in possession of Thomas Allen, Esq., of St. Louis.

## WM. RUSSELL.

ST. LOUIS, Oct. 1, 1847.

Slaves sometimes escaped and then were hunted down and severely punished. They had no rights under the law. *Courtesy of the Library of Congress*

The song "Run Children Run" is based on a field holler that slaves used while working in the plantation fields. (This song is on the Chicago Children's Choir CD that accompanies this book, *Songs on the Road to Freedom.*)

## RUN CHILDREN RUN

(Traditional)

*Run, children, run! Whoa, run, children, run!*
*Whoa, tell children run, I say*
*You got a right to the tree of life!*

*Little children, you've got a right*
*You've got a right, you've got a right*
*The Hebrew children got a right*
*With all them sorrows, you've got a right*
*You've got a right, you've got a right!*
*I've come to tell you, you got a right.*

*Children, run, you got a right*
*You got a right to the tree of life.*

As with many slave songs, "Run Children Run" carried a double meaning. The overseer heard only a work song. He did not hear the hidden meaning, so clear to the singers. They sang it as a hope for life with freedom. They sang it for brothers and sisters and friends who were running away. Then the words might be "Mary got the right to the tree of life" or "John got the right to the tree of life."

## Spirituals

While work songs and dances stayed close to the roots of African music, religious songs changed as African slaves converted to the Christian religion preached to them in America. *Spirituals* expressed their religious experience and longing. They also gave voice to the deep sorrow experienced in slavery and to the longing and determination for another life. They shouted hope in the face of despair. They brought people together, when the whole world tried to tear them apart.

Because slaves had no pianos or fiddles or organs, spirituals were sung a cappella. They clapped the rhythm or tapped their feet on the floor or ground. They swayed or danced to the music they made. The rhythms they clapped and stepped and sang came from Africa.

Like other songs with African origins, the spirituals frightened many white people. Singing these melodies was sometimes forbidden. Even religious services were sometimes banned. So slaves often met in secret. They sang and danced at night. They gathered in hidden places in the woods.

Spirituals, like field hollers, often carried coded messages. In some of them, a chariot or a train meant a way to freedom. "The Gospel Train" urged people to "get on board." The song promised, "there's room for many a'more." Slaves sang "Swing Low, Sweet Chariot." The chariot was coming "to carry me home." Home might be heaven—or it might be a safe refuge away from slavery.

The spiritual "Wade in the Water" comes from the biblical story of God "troubling the water" and healing the sick. As the music builds, the promise resounds: "God's gonna trouble the water." Who is going to be healed? The song talks about "children that Moses led" and "children of Israelites." The reference is to the biblical story of Moses leading the enslaved people of Israel to freedom. On one level, the song is a pious reference to the Bible. On another level, it is about freedom from slavery.

## WADE IN THE WATER

(Traditional)

*Chorus:*

*Wade in the water*
*Wade in the water, children*
*Wade in the water*
*God's gonna trouble the water.*

*Well, who are these children all dressed in red?*
*God's a-gonna trouble the water*

*Must be the children that Moses led*
*God's a-gonna trouble the water.*

*Chorus*

*Who's that young girl dressed in white?*
*Wade in the water*
*Must be the children of Israelites*
*God's gonna trouble the water.*

*Chorus*

*Jordan's water is chilly and cold*
*God's a-gonna trouble the water*
*It chills the body, but not the soul*
*God's a-gonna trouble the water.*

*Chorus*

*If you get there before I do*
*God's a-gonna trouble the water*
*Tell all of my friends I'm coming, too*
*God's a-gonna trouble the water.*

*Chorus*

Just as God had "troubled the water" and saved the "children that Moses led," so God would save them. Just as the water of the river Jordan "chills the body, but not the soul," their spirits would stay strong even if their bodies were beaten. And later, just as the words of the spiritual had given hope and strength to people living in—or escaping from—slavery, they would give hope and strength to people in the civil rights movement (see chapter 4).

## Lining the Song

Most slaves could not read and write. For a long time, they were forbidden to learn. Whipping, or worse, was the fate of any slave caught trying to read. That meant that songs and stories had to be learned in another way.

In the slaves' religious services, songs were often taught by repetition. The leader would sing one line of a song. This is called *lining the song*. Then the congregation would sing it back. This is called *raising the song*. This went on until the congregation learned the song.

Slaves were not the only people who learned by lining hymns. The practice began in Scotland in the 1500s. Presbyterian ministers needed a way to teach hymns to illiterate congregations. Lining hymns is also a way to teach songs to people who have no money for hymnbooks.

As people learned the songs, they invented harmonies. They repeated words and built refrains. Each song belonged to the people who sang it, on the day they sang it. Singing became intensely personal. At the same time, it strengthened community.

## Ring Shout

As in Africa, slaves used dance to express religious feeling. The *ring shout* was a kind of prayer. The dancers moved in a circle. They shouted and sang and danced, all at once. The ring shout had rules: The circle moved counterclockwise. Dancers did not cross their feet.

Some scholars say that the ring shout comes from Islamic tradition. They point out that the Arabic word *shaw't* means to move in a counterclockwise circle as part of a ritual performed at the Islamic holy city of Mecca. It may have been brought to America by slaves who were Muslims.

## Black and Beautiful: Finding Inspiration in Africa

In the mid–20th century in the United States, looking African was considered just about the opposite of looking beautiful. The standard of beauty was white beauty—blond and blue-eyed with silky, soft hair. For black Americans, looking good often required drastic measures. Men and women alike used hot combs or caustic chemicals to straighten naturally curly or kinky hair. Lighter skin meant greater beauty. So did facial features that looked more European than African.

Then came the civil rights movement of the 1960s. The movement brought a revolution in the way that black Americans saw themselves. Many stopped straightening their hair. They tried "natural" hairstyles. Big, bushy Afros, cornrows, and braids were black and beautiful. Wearing a *dashiki*, a loose-fitting African shirt, showed pride in black heritage. James Brown sang "Say It Loud—I'm Black and I'm Proud" (see chapter 6).

In the 1960s, Roger Wilkins was a young black lawyer in Washington, D.C. He looked at the movement toward black pride and the way that young activists were reconnecting with their African roots. "They were purging themselves of all that self-hate," Wilkins said, "asserting a human validity that did not derive from whites and pointing out that the black experience on this continent and in Africa was profound, honorable, and a source of pride."

Just as white Americans looked down on black Americans, they looked down on Africa. Even in the middle of the 20th century, textbooks ignored African achievement. They did not mention the wealth of the Songhai Empire. They said nothing about the University of Sankore. Stereotypes cast Africa as backward and "savage." In contrast, Europe was seen as the center of culture and learning.

At the same time that African Americans were challenging racism at home, Africans were challenging colonial domination and global racism. European nations ruled much of Africa. The French and British ruled the largest areas, from Egypt in the north to South Africa, from Tanganyika and Madagascar in the east to Senegal and Sierra Leone in the west. But in 1958, the African nation of Ghana won its independence. In 1963, Jomo Kenyatta became the first president of a free Kenya. A wave of independence movements swept away colonial rule.

In the United States, many of the young leaders of the civil rights movement found inspiration in Africa. John Lewis was a young leader of the Student Nonviolent Coordinating Committee (SNCC) and a participant in the first sit-ins to protest segregation (see chapter 5). He was elected to the U.S. Congress from Georgia in 1987. For over 20 years, he has been a strong voice for justice in Congress. Forty years after SNCC, he recalled the movement:

This wasn't even just an American movement anymore. Amazing changes were happening in Africa, where Ghana won its independence a year earlier, opening the door to a black African liberation movement that would soon sweep away much of the centuries-old colonial rule by European powers like Britain, Belgium, Portugal, and France. Zaire, Somalia, Nigeria, the Congo—freedom was stirring in all these places and we couldn't help being thrilled.

Musicians and dancers also connected with Mother Africa. Some traveled to Africa. Some lived and worked there for periods of time. Nitanju Bolade Casel joined a

West African dance company in the United States in 1972. Later, she traveled to Dakar, Senegal. She spent four years there, performing and learning and teaching. In 1985, she joined the musical group Sweet Honey in the Rock.

Sweet Honey itself has roots in both Africa and the civil rights movement. In her rap history of the group, Nitanju Bolade Casel says/sings:

> Great Black music is what we sing—a cappella style with a political ring. Using work songs, spirituals, gospel, and blues, the styles of Africa, jazz and love songs too; there is no limit to the sounds that we produce in a social commentary to express our views. Rock the rock in the rock, honey in the rock, Sweet Honey in the Rock.

Sweet Honey's songs weave together Africa and America, traditional and contemporary threads. For example, "The Little Shekere" is a rap song about the *shekere* gourd instruments of West Africa!

★　★　★　★　★

## Bernice Reagon Johnson and Sweet Honey in the Rock

Sweet Honey in the Rock was born out of the civil rights movement, mothered first by Bernice Reagon Johnson. Bernice was herself a child of the movement. She was born in a small town in Georgia in 1942. Her father was a minister, and Bernice grew up singing in the church. Until she was 13, her church had no piano. This early experience formed her a cappella singing style. A few years later, she sang at civil rights rallies. As in the church of her childhood, she could not count on having a piano, so she sang a cappella.

In 1961, Bernice was a student at Albany State College. With other college students, she committed her life to the civil rights movement. She was part of a small group of singers who led a mass rally at Albany's Mount Zion Baptist Church. Their singing "took the roof off" the church, keeping a captivated, energized rally going until after midnight.

During these early, heady organizing days at the beginning of the 1960s, Bernice encountered both the Student Nonviolent Coordinating Committee and her future husband, Cordell Reagon. He organized the SNCC Freedom Singers and Bernice joined the group.

In her junior year, Bernice was suspended from Albany State College for demonstrating. She transferred to Spelman College to continue studying voice and history. She earned a Ph.D. in

African American history from Howard University. In 1989, she won a MacArthur Fellowship, known as a "genius grant," to support her work for five years. She also worked for the Smithsonian Institution, where her projects included the 1994 production *Wade in the Water*, a 26-hour radio series cosponsored by National Public Radio.

Through her years of achievement and activism, Bernice's musical energy could not be contained. She made her first solo recording at the age of 19 and founded the Harambee Singers in Atlanta in 1966. Her singing was inseparable from her work in the civil rights movement. She sang in churches and at rallies and in jail. Years later, she wrote, "All of the energy of our living goes into our singing during our concerts. We are sharing so much more than a concert of songs. We are calling our people together. As a singer and a song leader, I draw upon the singing I sang in jail when singing was a bond. Singing gave us something to use as a weave and a connection."

After moving to Washington in 1971, Bernice gradually drew together a group of women singers who became Sweet Honey in the Rock. Though the members of the group change, their commitment to craft and to convictions remains solid. For over 30 years, this group of African American women has sung, danced, and inspired audiences around the world. Their singing is not just entertainment. They still move people to action for justice, just as the SNCC singers did during the movement's early days.

## Mother Africa Today

Today music from Africa travels around the world.

In West Africa, a *griot* was someone who kept the oral history of the people. The griots combined poetry and song in their presentations. They sang and told stories at the same time. They carried history and memory from one generation to the next. Their songs also commented on the life around them. Some griots continue the tradition today.

Rap and hip-hop music have roots in the griot tradition. Like the griots, rap musicians use a combination of spoken word and music. Their songs have strong rhythms. They tell stories of the life around them. Often they offer criticism of the way society is organized.

The roots of Afro-Cuban and Afro-Brazilian music are evident right in their names. Large numbers of African slaves were brought to both Cuba and Brazil. Like Africans in the United States, the descendants of slaves in Cuba and Brazil have unique cultural heritages. Afro-

Cubans have created distinctive music and art. Their culture combines African and Cuban influences. Afro-Brazilians combine African and Brazilian influences.

Such musical styles have been called *world music*. In the 21st century, music travels quickly around the world. U.S. audiences rock out to the music of Nigerian musician Femi Kuti. They celebrate the life and mourn the death of South African rapper Lucky Dube.

Ibé Kaba is a poet and spoken-word artist who immigrated to the United States from Africa. "I heard music was in the air," he wrote of an African musician in a U.S. club. "I heard hip hop had boomeranged back to the west coast of Africa and back." Kaba praises the "intersection between African and American . . . between reggae and hip hop . . . between hip hop past and future."

World music is one name for the international music scene. Since the 1980s, world music has become big business.

David Byrne is a founder of the band Talking Heads. He criticized the "world music" trend. Byrne thinks that calling some music "world music" shows disrespect. Calling something "world music" puts it in a box. This is music that is "not like us." World music is "exotic and therefore cute, weird but safe." That makes it not as real or not as important as mainstream music.

Even though he criticizes the term, Byrne loves the music. He thinks that learning to love the music of other cultures is important. He hopes that loving the music of another culture helps people to respect that culture.

The Sierra Leone Refugee All Stars show how music can build bridges. They are singers without a country. One band member had an arm cut off by rebels. Another had a hand amputated. Fleeing war and persecution, they began singing in a refugee camp in Guinea. There they were discovered by Canadian filmmakers. By 2007, they were touring the world.

"I think people only get the negative stories from Africa, and we had really positive experiences," said Zach Niles, one of the filmmakers.

> We had made great friends, we loved the food, and we especially loved the music. So when we came back and we tried to explain that to friendsĬ, they got this blank look because all they've seen are the horror stories. The wars and the famine and all those realities do exist, but there's so much depth to everything else in Africa.

His partner, Banker White, emphasized the importance of music in their message.

> Music is not only an important carrier of culture, it also expresses so many emotions, and we wanted to bring this kind of personal emotional connection to the project. It was really important to us that when audiences saw the film they felt like they were emotionally connecting with other people who—even though they've been through

these horrible, unthinkable experiences—they can still connect with on an emotional level, with a shared sense of humanity.

From reggae to rock 'n' roll, from rappers to refugees, African roots continue to nourish world music. The civil rights movement connected people from around the world. Some came together in the marches and demonstrations of the 1960s in the United States. Others found inspiration to work for justice or freedom in their own countries.

The civil rights movement emphasizes what people have in common. It teaches about the equality of all people. It reaches out to make connections among them. Like the movement, music speaks to people in many parts of the world. Often, it brings them together in movements for justice.

## Chapter 3

# The Civil Rights Movement: The Early Days

*We have come over a way that with tears has been watered*

*We have come, treading our path through the blood of the slaughtered*

*Out from the gloomy past, till now we stand at last*

*Where the white gleam of our bright star is cast.*

When did the civil rights movement begin? Many think it began in the 1960s. Others date it to 1954, when the Supreme Court said that school segregation was illegal. Others choose 1955, when Rosa Parks was arrested on an Alabama bus. In fact, the civil rights movement has a long history.

Black people have struggled for justice ever since they first came to North America. In colonial days, they made common cause with white indentured servants and with Native Americans. The first man to die in the Revolutionary War was Crispus Attucks, a free black man. Powerful black voices, such as that of Frederick Douglass, spoke out against slavery before the Civil War.

After the Civil War, amendments to the U.S. Constitution ended slavery and guaranteed equal rights to all. During the next few years, black people seized their new freedom. Across the South, they set up schools for children and adults. Some ran for political office, and won. White people in the South fought back. They made state

laws that restricted freedom for black people. Vigilante groups, people taking the law into their own hands, attacked, beat, and murdered black people. Throughout it all, black men and women resisted white efforts to keep them down.

## Ida B. Wells

The life of black teacher, journalist, and activist Ida B. Wells shows how this resistance continued. In 1884, Wells was a 25-year-old schoolteacher. She was ordered into a segregated, crowded train car. As she later wrote in her autobiography:

I refused, saying that . . . as I was in the ladies' car, I proposed to stay. [The conductor] tried to drag me out of the seat, but the moment he caught hold of my arm I fastened my teeth in the back of his hand. I had braced my feet against the seat in front and was holding to the back, and as he had already been badly bitten he didn't try it again by himself. He went forward and got the baggage man and another man to help him and of course they succeeded in dragging me out.

The law—the 1875 Civil Rights Act—was on her side. She sued the railroad, but the courts refused to enforce the law's ban on segregation. The power of prejudice was stronger than the law. This pattern was to continue for at least another century. Even when the law ordered equal rights, black people were denied.

Soon, throughout the South, the laws were changed to uphold segregation. The new laws that made segregation legal were called *Jim Crow laws*. The Jim Crow system of enforced segregation separated blacks and whites in almost all areas of life. The Supreme Court upheld the Jim Crow system. It said that segregation was legal. The key case was *Plessy v. Ferguson*, decided in 1896. Homer Plessy was black. He sued to end segregation on trains. He said that laws requiring racial segregation went against the Constitution. But the Supreme Court disagreed:

Laws permitting, or even requiring, separation . . . do not necessarily imply the inferiority of either race to the other. . . . We consider the underlying fallacy of the plaintiff's argument to consist in the assumption that the enforced separation of the two races stamps the colored race with a badge of inferiority. If this be so, it is not by reason of anything found in the act, but solely because the colored race chooses to put that construction upon it.

Segregation was bad, but it was only a small part of the story. Black people in the South lived under a reign of terror. The Ku Klux Klan and other hate groups used the threat of violence to keep black people from standing up for their rights, and to punish any black person who they thought had offended a white person. Sometimes the terror seemed almost random. Klansmen wearing hoods and white robes burned crosses in front of homes as a warning. They dragged black men out of their homes and beat them mercilessly.

The worst part of the reign of terror was *lynching*, when a mob punishes someone without due process of law. A lynch mob might beat its victims, or *tar and feather* them. That meant pouring hot, melted tar on a person and then sticking feathers in the tar. Often lynch mobs killed their victims, by hanging, beating, or burning them to death.

In the era of segregation, racists used lynching to remind all black people that they lived at the mercy of white people. Racist lynching happened most often in the South, but sometimes in the North as well. Lynching continued into the years of the civil rights movement. In 1955, 14-year-old Emmett Till was murdered in Mississippi for whistling at a white woman.

Ida B. Wells lost three friends to lynch mobs. In 1892, she worked in Memphis, Tennessee, as a journalist for the *Free Speech and Headlight* newspaper. Her friends Thomas Moss, Calvin McDowell, and Henry Stewart started the

Ida B. Wells fought for equal rights and led antilynching campaigns over 100 years ago. *Courtesy of the Library of Congress*

"People's Grocery Company." They were black, and a white-owned store lost customers to them. White men attacked the black grocers. Moss, McDowell, and Stewart fought back and shot one of the attackers. Then the three black men were arrested and jailed. A lynch mob broke into the jail. The mob dragged all three men out and murdered them.

Ida B. Wells wrote:

The city of Memphis has demonstrated that neither character nor standing avails the Negro if he dares to protect himself against the white man or become his rival. There is nothing we can do about the lynching now, as we are out-numbered and without arms. The white mob could help itself to ammunition without pay, but the order is rigidly enforced against the selling of guns to Negroes. There is therefore only one thing left to do; save our money and leave a town which will neither protect our lives and property, nor give us a fair trial in the courts, but takes us out and murders us in cold blood when accused by white persons.

Her friends' deaths launched Ida B. Wells on a life-long campaign against lynching. Her newspaper office in Memphis was destroyed after she wrote about the lynching. Then she moved to Chicago.

As the 20th century arrived, many black people were working for civil rights. Among them were the Johnson brothers. Together they produced "Lift Every Voice and Sing," the song still known as the "Negro National Anthem." Black poet James Weldon Johnson wrote the song in 1900. His brother, John Rosamond Johnson, wrote the music.

## LIFT EVERY VOICE AND SING

By James Weldon Johnson

*Lift every voice and sing*
*Till earth and heaven ring*
*Ring with the harmonies of Liberty*
*Let our rejoicing rise*
*High as the list'ning skies*
*Let it resound loud as the rolling sea.*
*Sing a song full of the faith that the dark past has taught us*
*Sing a song full of the hope that the present has brought us*
*Facing the rising sun of our new day begun*
*Let us march on till victory is won.*

*Stony the road we trod*

*Bitter the chast'ning rod*

*Felt in the days when hope unborn had died*

*Yet with a steady beat*

*Have not our weary feet*

*Come to the place for which our fathers sighed?*

*We have come over a way that with tears has been watered*

*We have come, treading our path through the blood of the*
*    slaughtered*

*Out from the gloomy past*

*Till now we stand at last*

*Where the white gleam of our bright star is cast.*


*God of our weary years*

*God of our silent tears*

*Thou who hast brought us thus far on the way*

*Thou who hast by Thy might*

*Led us into the light*

*Keep us forever in the path, we pray*

*Lest our feet stray from the places, our God, where we met*
*    Thee*

*Lest our hearts, drunk with the wine of the world, we forget*
*    Thee*

*Shadowed beneath Thy hand*

*May we forever stand*

*True to our God*

*True to our native land.*

Though the song reflects the tears and pain over the "gloomy past," each verse ends on a promise of hope. Fully aware of the difficulty of the task, the singers and organizers believe they will succeed. They know that the road to justice has been long—already measured in centuries. They remember the people who have died, honoring "the blood of the slaughtered." But they remain steadfast in faith, "true to our God, true to our native land." This song says clearly what many old spirituals said in code. Its words speak of life in the United States and of a struggle for justice. Its references are to the here and now, rather than to biblical stories. (You can listen to many versions of "Lift Every Voice and Sing" on YouTube.)

In 1905, just a few years after "Lift Every Voice and Sing" was written, Ida B. Wells joined with W. E. B. Dubois, a distinguished black intellectual and activist, and others in a series of meetings. The group of black leaders and some white allies became known as the Niagara Movement. Out of their meetings came a civil rights organization that is still strong a century later: *the National Association for the Advancement of Colored People (NAACP).*

The NAACP was founded in 1909. It began with a focus on fighting segregation and lynchings. Over the years, it became a leader in lawsuits challenging segregation. The NAACP emphasized working through the legal process and the political process. For information about the NAACP today, go to www.naacp.org.

Many different organizations worked for civil rights. They sometimes had differences over tactics or leadership, but they all contributed to the movement.

*The Urban League* was organized in 1910 in New York City as the Committee on Urban Conditions Among Negroes. Organized to provide social services to black people in northern cities, the Urban League became a full partner in the civil rights movement in the 1960s. For information about the Urban League today, go to www.nul.org.

*CORE, the Congress of Racial Equality,* was founded in Chicago in 1942 by an interracial group of students. Rather than legislation and lawsuits, CORE emphasized direct action. CORE staged the first sit-in in a Chicago restaurant in 1943, and the first Freedom Ride in 1947. For information about CORE today, visit www.core-online.org.

*The Montgomery Improvement Association* is best known for the Montgomery bus boycott. This was a local group in Montgomery, Alabama, that was organized around the bus boycott in 1956, and continued to do civil rights work through the 1960s.

*SCLC, the Southern Christian Leadership Conference,* also grew out of the Montgomery bus boycott. It was organized in 1957 to work nonviolently to end segregation. Dr. Martin Luther King Jr. was a founder and leader

## Negro, Black, and African American

In the early decades of the 20th century, the terms *black* and *Negro* were not considered dignified. They were terms used by slave traders and slave owners. Besides, many people of color are light-skinned, not black. At that time, *colored* was a respectful term. Later, *Negro* became the term preferred by black people for decades. During the 1960s, *black* became the preferred term. Some people, like long-time civil rights leader Roy Wilkins, continued to prefer the term *Negro* and refused to change. By the 1990s, many black people had adopted *African American* as their identity. They said that this name more accurately reflects their heritage.

31

of the SCLC. For information about the SCLC today, go to www.sclcnational.org.

SNCC, *the Student Nonviolent Coordinating Committee,* was organized by students in traditionally black southern colleges in 1960. SNCC (pronounced "snick") was the youngest, most radical civil rights organization. SNCC led the 1964 Mississippi Freedom Summer, often pushing other organizations to more radical action.

# The Scottsboro Boys

In 1931, the United States struggled in the Great Depression. Homeless people traveled across the country, looking for work. Some "rode the rails," hopping onto freight trains to travel without a ticket.

On March 25, 1931, about two dozen young people rode freight cars toward Memphis. A young white man stepped on the hand of a black man hanging onto the side of the train. A fight broke out. Most of the white youths were forced off the train. They said they had been attacked. The stationmaster telegraphed the next station. A group of armed men took nine black teens off the train. They also found two young white women riding the train. They questioned the white women. The women said they had been raped by the black teens.

Barely avoiding a lynching, the teens were tried 12 days later in Scottsboro, Alabama. They were represented by two court-appointed lawyers, both incompetent. The testimony at trial was contradictory and unconvincing. Some of the defendants were beaten until they "confessed." All were quickly found guilty. Eight of the nine were sentenced to death. Only 13-year-old Roy Wright was sentenced to life in prison.

Many people in the black community were outraged at the treatment of the Scottsboro Boys. Blues musician Huddy "Lead Belly" Ledbetter wrote and recorded a song called "Scottsboro Boys." Other people organized to work for their freedom. They found lawyers to appeal the guilty verdicts. The first organization to come to their legal defense was the U.S. Communist Party, through its International Labor Defense organization. They hired Samuel Liebowitz, an attorney with no communist connections, to represent the Scottsboro Boys in the retrial of their case.

The first guilty verdicts were overturned. For years, the Scottsboro Boys case continued to go back and forth through the courts. In one retrial, the jury handed down a guilty verdict, but Judge James Horton courageously set aside the jury's decision. He ordered another new trial. The judge's honesty led to his defeat in the next election.

Eventually, the truth came out: no one had raped the two girls. By then, many of the nine jailed teens had lost over a decade of their lives in jail. Some suffered assaults that left them permanently injured.

Among the people who worked for freedom for the Scottsboro Boys were 19-year-old Rosa Macauley and 29-year-old Raymond Parks. They met in 1931, as they organized for the Scottsboro Boys, and they were married the next year.

## Freedom to Ride

Raymond and Rosa Parks remained active in the civil rights movement. They lived in Montgomery, Alabama. Rosa worked as seamstress and housekeeper, and her husband was a barber. They were both active in the NAACP. Rosa Parks became an adviser to the NAACP youth council in Montgomery. In the summer of 1955, Rosa headed to the Highlander Folk School in Tennessee (soon to be known as the Highlander Center; see chapter 4). The school was dedicated to teaching activists how to work for justice. Highlander was integrated, a first experience of integration for many. Certainly, Rosa Parks did not experience integration back home in Montgomery.

Black people in Montgomery lived under segregation every day of the week. Restaurants were segregated. Schools were segregated. Jobs were segregated. The buses that people rode to their jobs were segregated. Sometimes that felt the worst, a twice-daily insult to hard-working people.

At that time, the front seats on the bus were reserved for white people. Most bus riders were black people. They

Rosa Parks attending a Highlander Christmas vacation event for black high school students in the mid-1950s. *Highlander Research and Education Center Records, Wisconsin Historical Society*

had to sit in the back. Sometimes, they also could sit in the middle section. A black person in the middle section had to stand or move to the back if a white person needed a seat. Often, black passengers were even prevented from walking through the white section of the bus. After they paid their fares at the front door of the bus, they would then be ordered to leave the bus and get back on through the back door. Sometimes the driver would drive away before they could reboard the bus.

For years, the NAACP had wanted to challenge bus segregation. They knew a challenge to bus segregation would be a tough case to win. They knew they had to have a strong case.

In March 1955, Claudette Colvin was arrested for refusing to move to the back of the bus. She was angry and ready to sue. NAACP leaders considered making hers the test case to challenge segregation.

Then they found out that Claudette was pregnant. She was 15 years old and unmarried. That meant many people would condemn her. Claudette's character, not segregation, would become the focus of arguments. They believed that a pregnant teenager would never get public support. The NAACP decided not to file a lawsuit based on her case. Reluctantly, they decided to wait for a "better" challenger to come along.

On December 1, 1955, Rosa Parks boarded a bus, going home from work. She sat down in the middle section. When more white passengers got on and filled the front seats, the driver told her to give up her seat and move farther back. She refused. She had not boarded the bus with the intention of being arrested, but in refusing his order, she acted with full consciousness and purpose. She knew she would be arrested. But she was not going to back down.

Rosa Parks knew the system was unjust, and she challenged it. Years later, in her autobiography, she wrote:

People always say that I didn't give up my seat because I was tired, but that isn't true. I was not tired physically, or no more tired than I usually was at the end of a working day. I was not old, although some people have an image of me as being old then. I was forty-two. No, the only tired I was, was tired of giving in.

Black leaders in Montgomery immediately began to organize. Friends from the NAACP paid the bail and got Rosa Parks out of jail the same evening. The NAACP worked more through the legal system than through mass action. NAACP lawyers filed court cases challenging segregation. Rosa Parks was an NAACP member, a law-abiding citizen, a woman on her way home from work. NAACP lawyers knew that her case would be the strongest case they could make against bus segregation.

Other people wanted to do more. The anger of black people over bus segregation and over the insults they suffered from bus drivers had been building up for years. They wanted the law to change, but they were not going to leave it to the lawyers.

The Women's Political Council included many strong and determined women. Some of them were professors at Alabama State College. They now decided to act. They met on the night of December 1 and wrote a letter urging a bus boycott. Long past midnight, the women worked, mimeographing tens of thousands of flyers calling for everyone to stop riding city buses. The next day, they began distributing the flyers.

Two days later, many black churches announced the boycott at services. They also announced *mass meetings*, where the community would gather to organize and support the protest. Ministers from the churches met and formed the Montgomery Improvement Association. This association would coordinate the boycott. A new minister had recently arrived in town. He was young—only 26 years old—but he was a good preacher. The Montgomery Improvement Association chose him to lead the boycott. His name was Martin Luther King Jr.

The bus boycott began in December 1955. The NAACP lawsuit was filed in February 1956. Rosa Parks was the main plaintiff. (A *plaintiff* is the person who sues someone else.) Three other plaintiffs were added to the lawsuit, including Claudette Colvin. The city of Montgomery was the defendant, defending its bus segregation laws. The lawsuit began to move slowly through the legal system.

For over a year, black people in Montgomery stayed off the buses. They walked to work. Some walked as far as 20 miles. They walked to church. They walked to the grocery store. Those who had cars shared rides. Black-owned cabs charged only bus fare for rides. Police arrested people

## Mass Meetings

The term *mass meeting* sounds like lots of people. Sometimes there were lots of people. In Montgomery during the bus boycott, the meetings were packed. Montgomery is a big city, so lots of people could come to the meetings. The bus boycott was a huge event, so lots of people wanted to be involved. When mass meetings were held in smaller communities, fewer people came. A *mass meeting* might be a dozen people.

Girls singing "Freedom Song" in a Selma church. Mass meetings were held to raise spirits and recruit participants for civil rights campaigns.
*Copyright 2008 by Matt Herron/TakeStock*

who shared rides. They arrested black cab drivers who did not charge regular rates.

At night, tired from walking, black people gathered in their churches. Dorothy Posey Jones played piano and organ at the First Baptist Church in Montgomery. Years later, she recalled that every seat was full during the bus boycott. The balcony and basement were filled, too. Singing and preaching at rallies restored people's energy. They sang songs of hope and faith and freedom.

A few white people supported the boycott. More opposed it. Some took violent action, bombing or burning black churches.

On January 30, 1956, Dr. Martin Luther King Jr. led a mass meeting at a church. A messenger interrupted the meeting. Dr. King's home had been bombed! His first question was for the safety of his wife, Coretta, and baby Yoki. No one knew whether they had been hurt. Dr. King rushed home to find them frightened but uninjured.

A crowd of black people gathered outside his home. Some wanted to take revenge for the bombing. Dr. King said no. He spoke to the crowd about nonviolence. He kept them from taking revenge.

*Nonviolence* means never acting with violence against any other person, even in self-defense. Dr. King preached

The Chicago Children's Choir toured the Rosa Parks Museum in Montgomery, Alabama, after giving a concert there. *Mary C. Turck*

and practiced nonviolence. For him, nonviolence was a religious and ethical commitment. He believed that nonviolence was necessary for the civil rights movement. Besides acting peacefully, he believed in the power of love. He preached about loving your enemies.

Not everyone was willing to sign on to nonviolence. Both love and nonviolence are difficult messages to hear or to preach, especially when someone is throwing bombs at your house. Under the leadership of Dr. King and others, the civil rights movement made a commitment to both principles.

Black people in Montgomery kept on despite the intimidation. They kept on walking during the day. Gathering for rallies, they kept on singing at night.

On November 13, 1956, the U.S. Supreme Court ruled that segregation on public buses was unconstitutional. The black people of Montgomery had won! The city tried to appeal, delaying for a few more weeks. The court rejected their attempt. On December 21, 1956, the triumphant black people of Montgomery boarded the buses, ending the boycott with victory.

Two years earlier, the Supreme Court had ruled that school segregation was unconstitutional. Neither the bus decision nor the school decision ended segregation. Only the stubborn, slow, steady work of tens of thousands of people could turn the law into reality.

## The Supreme Court Speaks, 1954

Black and white students in the South attended separate schools. State laws required segregation. Segregation meant more than separation. White students got better buildings, newer books, and more money for their schools. Black parents and students courageously demanded equality. The NAACP led the way. NAACP lawyers met with parents and students in many towns and cities. They sued for equal rights. In 1954, four of the NAACP cases went to the Supreme Court.

## Clarendon County, South Carolina

In 1950, Clarendon County was rural and poor. More than 22,000 of its 32,000 residents were black. Two-thirds of the black families earned less than $1,000 per year. Black adults had an average of less than four years of education.

The county's schools were strictly segregated. White students were bused to larger schools. There were no buses for black students. They attended one- or two-room schools scattered across the county. Most "colored" schools had no electricity or running water. Money flowed to white schools. Per-pupil spending on white students was four times higher.

Black children had to walk up to nine miles to get to school. Black parents first organized to ask for a school bus. The county refused. NAACP lawyers met with parents, and sued the county. Their lawsuit, filed in 1950, demanded desegregation.

## Farmville, Virginia

Barbara Johns was born in New York in 1935. Her parents had moved north, looking for work. They returned to Virginia while Barbara was still a child, and she grew up there. She helped out in her uncle's country store. Sometimes she picked cotton with her grandmother.

In 1951, Barbara was a junior at Moton High School in Farmville, Virginia. Some accounts call her shy and quiet. She belonged to the school chorus and to its New Homemakers of America group.

Moton was the black high school. Its buildings were old and run-down. It had been built for 180 students. Now it held almost 500. Sometimes three classes met in the auditorium at the same time. At least one class met on a school bus. The white high school—Farmville High—had a gymnasium, lockers, a cafeteria, and science equipment in its labs.

Over and over, black parents asked for a new school. The county made promises, but never kept them. Finally, the county built three tarpaper shacks alongside Moton High School. Moton's teachers built fires in wood stoves. Students shivered in their winter coats.

Barbara led a group of students in secret meetings. They decided to call a student strike to demand a new high school, equal to the white high school. On April 23,

1951, one of the students called the principal. Disguising his voice, he told the principal that the police were about to arrest two students downtown. Quickly, the principal left the building to rescue his students.

Next, the students delivered a note "from the principal" to all 25 classrooms. The note summoned everyone to an assembly in the auditorium. When everyone arrived, Barbara Johns appeared on the stage. She took off her shoe and pounded it on the podium for order. Her fellow organizers escorted teachers out of the room.

Speaking to the students, Barbara seemed anything but shy and quiet. She talked about the rickety school buses and the crowded conditions. "Look at the white school just down the road," she said. "The white students have a real gymnasium, up-to-date science labs, and shiny new buses." Barbara called on students to walk out in protest. And they did.

A mass meeting a few nights later drew more than a thousand people. Parents supported their children. The NAACP sent lawyers to meet with the group. The NAACP lawyers said they would not ask for a new high school. Instead, they explained, they would sue for an end to segregation. The students agreed, sweeping their parents along into a lawsuit that would make history.

## Topeka, Kansas

Across the country in Topeka, Kansas, a young girl named Linda Brown attended a black elementary school. She had to travel more than two miles to the segregated school. A white school was just four blocks from her home. Linda and her parents believed that she should be able to attend the school closest to her home. They agreed to become part of the NAACP's legal challenge to segregation. Their lawsuit was filed in 1951.

## New Castle County, Delaware

Claymont, Delaware, had a large, well-equipped high school—for whites only. Ethel Louise Belton lived in Claymont, but she could not go to high school there. Instead, she had to travel two hours daily to Wilmington, Delaware. Wilmington had the state's only high school for black students, Howard High School. Claymont's high school had more classes and activities than Howard.

Seven-year-old Shirley Bulah had to walk to her elementary school every day. Her Delaware school was for black students only. A school bus to the nearby whites-only school passed her house every day. She was not allowed to ride the bus. The white school had an auditorium, a basketball court, hot water, drinking fountains, a nurse's office, and adequate bathrooms. The black school had none of these.

Black parents and students wanted equality. The NAACP filed lawsuits demanding integration. Slowly, the lawsuits made their way through the court system.

Adults also studied in citizenship schools across the South. Because many black adults had not had the opportunity to complete school, the citizenship schools taught reading, writing, arithmetic, and the Constitution. *Ida Berman, Highlander Research and Education Center Records, Wisconsin Historical Society*

## Brown v. Board of Education

In 1954, the NAACP lawsuits challenging school segregation finally reached the Supreme Court of the United States. The lawsuits were consolidated. Together, they bore the name of *Brown v. Board of Education* (after Linda Brown, the plaintiff in the Topeka case). In 1954, the Supreme Court ruled on whether school segregation violated the Constitution of the United States.

State laws ordered segregation, but the Constitution is the highest law of the land. If a state law violates the Constitution, then the state law is invalid. The 14th Amendment was added to the Constitution after the Civil War. It was one of the laws that ended slavery and guaranteed equal rights to all persons.

### Fourteenth Amendment

Section. 1. All persons born or naturalized in the United States and subject to the jurisdiction thereof, are citizens of the United States and of the State wherein they reside. No State shall make or enforce any law which shall abridge the privileges or immunities of citizens of the United States; nor shall any State deprive any person of life, liberty, or property, without due process of law; nor deny to any person within its jurisdiction the equal protection of the laws.

The highest court in the country ruled that the 14th Amendment prohibited school segregation. Supreme Court chief justice Earl Warren wrote: "Does segregation of children in public schools solely on the basis of race, even though the physical facilities and other 'tangible' factors may be equal, deprive the children of the minority group of equal education opportunities? We believe that it does." Ordering that school segregation end, he continued: "Separate educational facilities are inherently unequal."

The Supreme Court said that segregated schools were *inherently* unequal. Even if segregated white and black

Rosalind Silverman of New York teaches children music in a Baptist church in Farmsville, Virginia, July 18, 1963. *Associated Press*

schools had equal buildings, equal books, equal buses, they would still be unequal. The very fact of racial segregation implied that black people were less than whites. The fact of segregation made them unequal.

*Brown v. Board of Education* ordered an end to segregated schools, but segregation did not end. The court said that state governments could take time to desegregate their schools. It said they could act "with all deliberate speed." Southern governments resisted acting at all. They refused to follow the law of the land.

Prince Edward County, Virginia, closed its schools in May 1959 rather than integrate them. White children attended private, segregated schools, paid for by the county. Black children had nowhere to go.

## Little Rock, 1957

In Little Rock, Arkansas, in 1957, nine black students tried to enroll in the previously all-white high school. A federal court ordered the school to let them in. Arkansas Governor Orval Faubus said they could not enroll. He called out the Arkansas National Guard to stop them. U.S. President Dwight D. Eisenhower told Faubus he

Dorothy Counts, the first black student to attend Harding High School in Charlotte, North Carolina, tries to maintain her poise as she's taunted by shouting, gesticulating white students, September 4, 1957. *Associated Press*

could not disobey the court. Eisenhower said Faubus could not use the National Guard to keep the students out. Instead, the National Guard had to protect the teenagers.

On September 14, the nine teens tried to enter the school. Governor Faubus ordered the National Guard troops to leave. The teens were left at the mercy of a mob. White adults surrounded them, screaming and throwing bricks. Local police evacuated the students.

Then President Eisenhower sent in federal troops. He sent the 101st Airborne Division paratroopers. He also

Some of the first pioneers to cross the color line were young children and teenagers. President Dwight D. Eisenhower sent U.S. Army troops to enforce school integration in Little Rock, Arkansas. The soldiers escorted nine African American students past threatening mobs at Central High School in September 1957. *Associated Press*

put the Arkansas National Guard under federal control. The troops protected the students as they entered and left the school. Each student had a guard to protect him or her inside the school. In a letter to the parents of the Little Rock Nine, the president wrote, "I believe that America's heart goes out to you and your children in your present ordeal. In the course of our country's progress toward equality of opportunity, you have shown dignity and courage in circumstances which would daunt citizens of lesser faith."

For the rest of the year, the military protected the students. The following year, Governor Faubus ordered all state high schools closed. This was the only way he could keep black students out. When Arkansas high schools reopened in 1959, they finally were integrated.

Across the South, integration proceeded, school by school. Little Rock got headlines in part because the president and the governor opposed each other. In other towns and schools, few people were watching. Students braved threats and intimidation. Parents backed them up. The courage of thousands of students and parents defeated segregation.

Whites rallied at the state capitol to oppose integration of Little Rock schools. *John T. Bledsoe, courtesy of the Library of Congress*

## Chapter 4

# Singing in the Churches

# Joshua fought the Battle of Jericho
# And the walls came tumblin' down

Gospel music and spirituals were growing-up music for many African American civil rights activists. Many of them were religious people, and many of the movement's leaders were also religious leaders. Ministers, nuns, priests, and rabbis marched for civil rights. And, as mentioned in chapter 1, civil rights meetings often took place in southern churches.

Many religious people defended the human rights of all people. They brought their stories and their beliefs into the civil rights movement. The Bible's story of the Jews' exodus from slavery was familiar to both Christian and Jewish Americans. The prophets of Jewish scripture cried out for justice. The Christian Gospels preached about loving your enemies and embracing nonviolence. And religious songs expressed this longing for freedom, justice, and peace. So it is not surprising that many religious songs became movement songs.

## Fisk Jubilee Singers Take Spirituals to the World

In 1865, the Civil War ended and slavery was abolished. The next year, Fisk University opened in Nashville, Tennessee. It offered a liberal arts education to "young men and women irrespective of color." The new university had little money. Its wealth was in its people. They were its treasures.

George White was one of those people. White was a Union Army veteran. He had been a choirmaster and a band sergeant. Now he was a missionary from New York. He was committed to building a university that would welcome black people. He became the new school's treasurer and music professor.

Ella Sheppard was another treasure. She was a former slave. Her father, also a slave, had purchased his own freedom and then his daughter's, and taken her away to Ohio.

Now she enrolled at Fisk to become a teacher. Ella was also a musician. At the age of 18, she became Fisk's first black teacher and its assistant choir director.

From the very beginning, Fisk was falling apart. There was no money to repair the old buildings. There was no money for anything. Though tuition was only $12 a year, students did not have even that much. Besides the money problems, Fisk came under attack from the Ku Klux Klan. A student was shot at. Others were beaten and whipped.

George White spent his own savings to keep the school going. He and Ella Sheppard planned a concert tour to raise money for the college. On October 6, 1871, they gathered a few of the Fisk music students and took them north. At first, their way was hard. They did not have coats for the northern chill. They were turned away from hotels because they were black. They barely made enough to cover costs.

The singers started by singing classical music. Gradually, they added "cabin music," the songs that were sung by slaves in their cabins on the plantations of the South. They also added spirituals.

Ella Sheppard wrote:

> The slave songs were associated with slavery and the dark past, and represented the things to be forgotten. They were sacred to our parents. We did not dream of ever using them in public. It was only after many months that gradually our hearts were opened to the wonderful beauty and power of our songs.

In Oberlin, Ohio, the tide turned. Their spirituals won the hearts of audiences. They took a new name: "Jubilee Singers." The name came from the Bible. Chapter 25 of the Book of Leviticus speaks of the jubilee year—a year of freedom and forgiveness of debts.

The Jubilee Singers began making money on tour. They raised enough money to support the college.

They still met with prejudice. The *New York World* newspaper called them "trained monkeys." But their support grew. In 1872, they performed at the White House. In 1873, they toured Europe.

Fisk University still struggled. Across the South, angry mobs burned schools that educated black people. At one point, the army had to guard the Fisk campus. But it survived.

## From Spirituals to Gospel Music

For over 200 years, spirituals belonged to African Americans, in and out of slavery. Spirituals belonged to the people, not just to musicians. They belonged to congregations, not to performers and audiences. Songs were lined out for people to learn. Singers invented their own harmonies as they sang.

In the 1920s and 1930s, *gospel music* appeared. Black gospel music grew out of the tradition of spirituals, but unlike spirituals, gospel songs were written by individual composers. Gospel musicians wrote down their music. They composed harmonies. They performed for an audience.

The Reverend Charles Tindley (1851–1933) was the first composer to copyright gospel songs. He composed more than 60 songs, and he is often called the Father of Gospel Music.

Reverend Dr. C. J. Johnson was born into a musical family in 1913. His father taught shape note singing. (*Shape notes* are a way of writing music used in many churches, especially in the South. Notes of different pitch are represented by different shapes, rather than just different positions on a musical staff.) Johnson's grandmother sang lined-out hymns and spirituals. He was raised by his grandmother. Dr. Johnson described his grandmother strutting down the aisle of Mount Moriah Baptist Church in Atlanta, singing "One Morning Soon."

At the age of five, Johnson led his first song in church. He preached a sermon when he was 10 years old. He was ordained a minister in the Missionary Baptist Church. He could have continued as a preacher without further education, but he wanted more. In 1959, at the age of 46, he completed a doctorate in religion.

Dr. Johnson was a Baptist minister and also a songwriter and singer. He tells a childhood story of composing a song:

> I was on a bus going to work, and a white man asked me to move out of my seat. I was already in the back, and I refused. When he tried to physically move me, I bit him. I was thrown off the bus by the driver, and he continued to ride. As I walked to work all the way across town, I felt like I wanted to leave this place. I did not want to stay in a place like this. As soon as I got to work, I wrote this song, "I Wanna Go Where Jesus Is."

Years later, in 1970, his song won a gold record, meaning that it sold one million copies.

Thomas A. Dorsey is also called the Father of Gospel Music. His father was a Baptist preacher and his mother a church organist. As a child, he learned to play the piano and organ from his mother. He played church music at church and any music he liked at home. Dorsey said he started composing music at the age of eight and could not imagine life without music. In his early professional life, he sang blues music as "Georgia Tom." He became popular and successful. Then he experienced a kind of breakdown. Recovering, he turned to religion.

As he had composed blues, now Dorsey composed gospel songs. Gospel music featured strong rhythms and choral arrangements. Many songs were arranged for quartets or small groups. They also featured solos. Many of

Dorsey's gospel songs had syncopated notes in an eight-bar blues structure.

In the 1920s, Dorsey's songs scandalized some church people. They thought the strong rhythms of gospel made the music unfit for churches. Some pastors called it "the devil's music." Years later Dorsey said, "I've been thrown out of some of the best churches in America."

By 1931, Dorsey had found a church home in Chicago. He organized the world's first gospel chorus at Chicago's Ebenezer Baptist Church. Then he moved to Pilgrim Baptist Church to start a choir there. Dorsey led Pilgrim's gospel choirs for decades. He composed hundreds of gospel songs. In 1932, tragedy struck. His wife died in childbirth, along with their son. The heartbroken Dorsey wrote "Precious Lord, Take My Hand." In later years, this song became the favorite of Dr. Martin Luther King Jr. (This song is on the Chicago Children's Choir CD that accompanies this book, *Songs on the Road to Freedom*.)

The Reverend Charles Tindley and Thomas Dorsey may be the fathers of gospel music, but Mahalia Jackson is its queen. Born in New Orleans in 1911, she became an orphan at the age of six. Her Aunt Duke raised "Halie" and her brother with hard work and whippings. Though she hardly had time for school, Halie could go to church. Singing her heart out, she found comfort there.

With thousands of other black people, Mahalia Jackson took part in the Great Migration of the 1920s (see chapter 6). She moved from New Orleans to Chicago. She began singing with a professional gospel group. Her incredible voice brought continuing success. Many people wanted her to "cross over" and sing nonreligious music. This would have brought even more money and fame. Jackson refused. Throughout her life she kept her commitment to sing only religious songs. But she did move beyond churches. World tours took her to concert halls in Europe, Africa, Japan, and India. She sometimes toured with Thomas Dorsey.

Jackson also sang for the civil rights movement. She was the only woman on stage at the 1963 March on Washington. She sang at Dr. Martin Luther King Jr.'s funeral. She sang his favorite hymn, "Precious Lord, Take My Hand."

## Religious Music in the Movement

For people fighting for civil rights, however, singing was not just a performance by the people standing at the front of the room. Everybody sang, participating in the music as they did in the movement. Every rally, every march, every mass meeting included singing. People sang songs as they met and as they marched and as they sat in jail. *Song leaders* might get out front to introduce the songs and guide the singing, but everybody joined with them.

"Music, as I saw it and still see it, is used in different ways," says Hollis Watkins, a SNCC song leader (see chapter 5). "Number one, music is used to motivate people. Music is used to inspire people. Music is used also to educate through sending messages to people."

Singing together, people felt closer to one another. That closeness gave them strength. "That sets the stage," Watkins explains.

> After having created this bonding and unifying process, helping people to feel good . . . now you can talk about realities. That's where—after having sung freedom songs—we would talk about the importance of voter registration. . . . [Music] set the stage and tone for people to really get involved and understand why they need to be involved.

The leaders often began with familiar church songs. Sometimes they sang the songs as they always had. The spirituals' hidden messages, which had once moved slaves to hope for freedom and a better life, now inspired African Americans to fight for racial justice.

One spiritual that became popular for its hidden message of hope was "The Battle of Jericho." (This song is on the Chicago Children's Choir CD that accompanies this book, *Songs on the Road to Freedom*.) The song comes from a Bible story found in the Book of Joshua. In the story, Joshua commanded the Israelite army. The enemy was in the walled city of Jericho. They seemed invincible. God

come let us build a new world together

STUDENT NONVIOLENT COORDINATING COMMITTEE 8½ RAYMOND STREET, N.W. ATLANTA 14, GEORGIA

A SNCC poster used a photo by Danny Lyon showing SNCC workers kneeling in prayer. For many people in the movement, action grew from religious conviction. *McCain Library and Archives, University of Southern Mississippi*

commanded Joshua to march around the city with the priests and the people. They marched once every day for six days. On the seventh day, they marched around the city seven times. They blew their trumpets and shouted. The walls of the city "came tumbling down."

Like the Israelites, civil right activists faced strong enemies. But they believed that God was on their side. The spirituals voiced their faith in God and in their ultimate victory. The song reminded them that victory does not always go to the strong.

Phillip Armstrong started singing early. His father sang in the church choir at St. Benedict the African East in Chicago. He took four-year-old Phillip up to the choir with him. Though it was an adult choir, they made an exception for Phillip. By the age of six, he joined the choir officially. He got his first solo when he was 10 or 11 years old. As a high school student, he serves as junior choir director for the church.

"Especially with me expressing my religion," Phillip says, "gospel is my passion. I love jazz and all kinds of music, but gospel is my background."

Music opened doors for Phillip, both at his church and in the wider world. Joining the Chicago Children's Choir opened new doors and offered new opportunities.

Phillip believes that the civil rights movement is still needed. "Racism and a lot of things are present today. It may not be just against blacks, but it could be against any kind of orientation or any kind of race or ethnicity. As a young generation, we need to fight for what is right."

For him, music is a part of that fight. While gospel music is his passion, he believes that different kinds of music touch different people. "Music is something people use every day in our life," Phillip says. "It's universal and everybody can relate to it in many ways. . . . In my music life, I will always want to create music that will relate to everyone, not just one type of setting, like religious, but all people."

Phillip Armstrong. *Mary C. Turck*

**"As a young generation, we need to fight for what is right."**

50

## THE BATTLE OF JERICHO

(Traditional)

Chorus:

*Joshua fought the battle of Jericho, Jericho, Jericho*
*Joshua fought the battle of Jericho*
*And the walls came tumbling down.*

*You may talk about your men of Gideon*
*You may talk about your men of Saul*
*But there's none like good old Josh-u-a*
*At the battle of Jericho.*

Chorus

*Joshua rose early in the morning*
*That is when the trumpets blew*
*They marched around the city*
*At the battle of Jericho.*

Chorus

*Right up to the walls of Jericho*
*He marched with spear in hand*
*Joshua commanded the children to shout*
*And the walls came a tumblin' down, down, down, down.*

Chorus

Sometimes activists invented new words or verses for the old songs. Song leaders often lined the songs to intro-

duce the new lyrics. The leader would sing a new line to make the song fit the time and place, and the protesters would repeat it. For example, a traditional civil rights song is "Ain't Gonna Let Nobody Turn Me Around." (This song is on the Chicago Children's Choir CD that accompanies this book, *Songs on the Road to Freedom*.) In Alabama in the 1960s, Governor George Wallace preached segregation. A civil rights leader would sing "Ain't Gonna Let George Wallace Turn Me Around." In Chicago, the song became "Ain't Gonna Let Mayor Daley Turn Me Around." Vietnam War protesters targeted Secretary of State Henry Kissinger. They sang "Ain't Gonna Let Henry Kissinger Turn Me Around."

In Selma, Alabama, people marched to demand voting rights and an end to segregation. They invented new words for "The Battle of Jericho."

## MARCHING 'ROUND SELMA

*Marching 'round Selma like Jericho, Jericho, Jericho*
*Marching 'round Selma like Jericho*
*For segregation wall must fall.*

*Look at people answering*
*To the freedom fighters call*
*Black, brown, and white American say*
*Segregation must fall.*

*Good evening freedom's fighters*
*Tell me where you're bound*

The Chicago Children's Choir marching across the historic Edmund Pettus Bridge. After an emotional visit to the Slavery Museum in Selma, they could not keep from singing. *Mary C. Turck*

*Tell me where you're marching*
*"From Selma to Montgomery town."*

When the spiritual "Oh, Mary, Don't You Weep" was rewritten by Charles Neblett, it became one of the most famous songs of the movement. The new words speak about many aspects of the civil rights struggle. The title and first verse talk about desegregating buses. By the last verse, the struggle moves to desegregating jobs. The singer is not just going to ride at the front of the bus—he is going to drive it! In between, verses touch on voting, on desegregating schools and stores, on going to jail, and even on swimming in public pools.

## If You Miss Me from the Back of the Bus

Lyrics by Charles Neblett, traditional music

*If you miss me from the back of the bus*
*And you can't find me nowhere*
*Come on up to the front of the bus*
*I'll be riding up there*

Chorus (changes with each verse):

*I'll be riding up there, Lord*
*I'll be riding up there*
*If you miss me from the back of the bus*
*I'll be riding up there*

*If you miss me from Jackson State*
*And you can't find me nowhere*
*Come on over to Ole Miss*
*I'll be studying over there*

Repeat last line as chorus

*If you miss me from the cotton fields*
*And you can't find me nowhere*
*Come on down to the courthouse*
*I'll be voting right there*

Repeat last line as chorus

*If you miss me from the Thrifty Drug Store*
*And you can't find me nowhere*

*Come on over to Woolworth's*
*'Cause I'll be sitting in there*

*Repeat last line as chorus*

*If you miss me from the picket line*
*And you can't find me nowhere*
*Come on down to the jailhouse*
*I'll be rooming down there*

*Repeat last line as chorus*

*If you miss me from the Mississippi River*
*And you can't find me nowhere*
*Come on down to the municipal plunge*
*'Cause I'll be swimming in there*

*Repeat last line as chorus*

*If you miss me from the front of the bus*
*And you can't find me nowhere*
*Come on up to the driver's seat*
*I'll be driving up there*

*Repeat last line as chorus*

Songs with religious roots were especially important to older members of the movement. Many older people were nervous about taking a political stand. The religious roots of the movement and of its songs gave them courage and made the struggle seem "right." Hollis Watkins explains:

Hollis Watkins and Arvenna Adams sing freedom songs to celebrate the release of ministers and students jailed for attempting to integrate churches in Jackson, Mississippi. *Copyright 1978 Matt Herron/Take Stock*

If it was at a mass meeting, and you had more older people there, you probably would start out by singing some of the songs they were familiar with. Especially if you got a lot of people who may not know the songs initially, you would start out with songs that they were familiar with, that they sang at church. You would sing a few verses just the way they sang at church. Then you would explain, "We're going to change a couple words and make them fit in with our movement." And then you would change a few words.

The church song goes:

*Who's that yonder dressed in white?*
*Must be the children of the Israelite.*

And then you change it to:

*Who's that yonder dressed in white?*
*Must be the children fighting for their equal rights.*

Then they would see it and understand it. You start with something they can relate to and then explain the changing of the words.

## "We Shall Overcome"

One song evolved from its origins in the world of spirituals and gospel music to become the anthem of the civil rights movement. That song is "We Shall Overcome." No other song is so close to people's hearts. No other song has such a close identity with the movement. (This song is on the Chicago Children's Choir CD that accompanies this book, *Songs on the Road to Freedom.*)

"We Shall Overcome" has a complicated history. Probably different parts of the song came from different places. Different people sang it over time. Like many songs, it came from "the people" rather than from a single composer.

Part of the melody of "We Shall Overcome" may date back to slavery days. Some believe that it came from the spiritual "No More Auction Block for Me." The auction block was the place where slaves were bought and sold.

Slaves had no voice in their future. A slave owner could sell any of them at any time.

"No More Auction Block for Me" expressed hope. Parents hoped that their children would not be sold away to another state, a faraway plantation, a cruel master. They hoped that they themselves would not be sold away from their children. They hoped for an end to the buying and selling of human beings, an end to slavery.

Other people think "We Shall Overcome" started out as a song sung by slaves as they worked in the fields. The song's refrain was "I'll be all right."

In the early 20th century a Methodist minister named Charles Albert Tindley wrote down a gospel hymn called "I'll Overcome Some Day." Tindley was not the composer of the song. He wrote down a song that already existed—perhaps one based on the slave songs discussed above. However "We Shall Overcome" began life, it grew and changed with the times like the movement for freedom itself.

After World War II, black women at a tobacco plant in Charleston, South Carolina, organized a union. They wanted better wages and working conditions. The bosses, the police, and most of the town were more than unfriendly. The women were in danger of losing their jobs, going to jail, or worse. One day, the women workers were standing outside the plant in the rain. One of them began to sing Reverend Tindley's song. She changed the words, singing "we" instead of "I." Then they invented a new verse: "We will win our rights." And they did.

Pete Seeger has been singing and organizing for 70 years. He is pictured here at the Highlander Center, one of many places where he put his music at the service of the civil rights movement. *Highlander Research and Education Center Records, Wisconsin Historical Society*

After the strike, two of the women went to the Highlander Center, a school for organizers in Tennessee. It was a most unusual place. Black people and white people studied together. In their own communities, they were not allowed to live or study or work side by side. At the Highlander Center, they were equals. Government officials and police did not like the Highlander Center. They thought it was subversive, possibly communist.

The two women from South Carolina taught their song to folks at the Highlander Center. Zilphia Horton, a teacher at Highlander, taught the song to Pete Seeger. Seeger had a magazine called *People's Songs*, which was published in New York. He printed the song there as "We Will Overcome" in 1947.

One night in 1957, a local white sheriff led a bunch of men to the Highlander School. They turned off the electricity so everyone inside was in the dark. They forced the people at the school to lie on the floor. They broke up furniture and searched for evidence of "communism."

Jamalia Jones was one of the students lying on the floor in fear and darkness. She was 13 years old. She was afraid, and she wanted not to be afraid. So she began singing the song "We Shall Overcome," and she made up a new verse. She sang, "We are not afraid." Her friends joined in. For two hours, they sang. Finally, the sheriff and the men left them alone.

The song grew and traveled, taking on a life of its own. A young musician named Guy Carawan learned the song and took it on the road. In 1960, Carawan taught "We Shall Overcome" to young people who were meeting to found the Student Nonviolent Coordinating Committee. People in the civil rights movement claimed it as their anthem. They sang it as they sat in at segregated lunch counters. They sang it at rallies and at marches. They sang it as they were beaten and arrested and jailed. They sang it at funerals for those who were murdered because they had worked for civil rights and justice.

Eventually, the song moved around the world. Demonstrators sang it in South Africa, protesting against the racist apartheid system of that country. In China, demonstrators in Tiananmen Square sang it as they put their lives on the line for freedom. In Northern Ireland, Catholics and Protestants fought deadly, bitter battles. Those who sought peace in Northern Ireland sang "We Shall Overcome."

## Sacred Music and Secular Times

Many black musicians moved from roots in sacred music to success in secular markets. Aretha Franklin is known as the Queen of Soul (see chapter 6). She began singing in her father's church. Her father, the Reverend C. L. Franklin, was one of the best-known black preachers in the 1950s and 1960s. He had his own radio show. Many famous singers visited his home and church. So did Dr. Martin Luther King Jr.

Choir artistic director Josephine Lee reflected on the choir's Freedom Tour of the civil rights sites. "I had never been to the South," she said. "For me, it was paramount that we go on this tour. As an opportunity to open our eyes, share our music, and connect with community—to be able to connect with the mission of the choir and to witness firsthand with these singers and to be able to reflect and to heal some of the past and to learn from our history and move forward.

"Performing 'We Shall Overcome' at the 16th Street Baptist Church in Birmingham, there was so much connection. [It felt like singing] that we haven't forgotten. We are living proof that people who died before us did not die in vain. Our children are here to continue that legacy and to promote freedom."

Artistic director Josephine Lee conducts the Chicago Children's Choir at the Civil Rights Museum in Memphis. *Davin Peelle*

**"We are living proof that people who died before us did not die in vain."**

Many movement songs come from Christian churches. Yet even people who are not Christian, or not religious, still sing them. What do they feel? What do the songs mean to them?

Anne Wildman graduated from the Chicago Children's Choir in 2007. As a nonbeliever, she thought about singing religious songs. "It's no fun to sing a song that's about something I can't relate to at all," Anne said. "After I thought about it, I could relate to them.

"I don't think of it in a religious context. I think of it in a human, mortal context. We are all a part of something; we all exist here together. I don't believe that we are a part of God's body, but I can interpret that in my own, nonreligious way. In a lot of ways, I think it means the same thing to me as to people who are religious.

"It seems to me that almost every religious, spiritual song can be interpreted in a humanistic way. We all need something from each other. We all are connected, not necessarily in a spiritual way, but we are all human and we all share that and we all share the world we live in and the time we are here. So the songs always have that message and that power for me."

**"It seems to me that almost every religious, spiritual song can be interpreted in a humanistic way."**

Rosa Parks (*left*) joins hands and sings with Coretta Scott King (*center*), widow of slain civil rights leader Dr. Martin Luther King Jr., and Myles Horton, founder and director of the Highlander School and Conference Center in Tennessee, October 13, 1988. Ms. Parks had a room in the Martin Luther King Center in Atlanta dedicated in her name. *Associated Press*

In the 1960s, Aretha began singing professionally. She crossed over from gospel music to popular music. As she became a bigger and bigger star, she continued to support the civil rights movement. She sang at events supporting Dr. King and the struggle.

Mavis Staples also sings both sacred and secular music. During her childhood years, she spent her summers with her grandmother in Mississippi. She remembers going to little churches that had no organ or piano. She says that the music in these churches "has soul in it, the spirit of the people." That spirit comes out in gospel songs, and in secular songs, too.

## SNCC: Freedom Singers and Freedom Song

Like Mavis Staples, the SNCC Freedom Singers show the way that sacred music moved across the divide to inspire people of many faiths or of no religion at all. These talented young singers met as members of the Student Nonviolent Coordinating Committee. They marched together, sang together, and went to jail together.

One night in Albany, Georgia, in 1961, people gathered at the Mount Zion Baptist Church for a mass meeting. Bernice Johnson and Cordell Reagon and a few other young people stood up front to lead the singing. People sang along. People cried. People stood and linked arms, swaying and singing. The mass meeting lasted past midnight. No one wanted to leave. The SNCC Freedom Singers had been born. For hundreds of rallies and meetings, the SNCC singers led the music and chose the songs.

Many SNCC members had roots in southern religious traditions, but others did not. They all shared a commitment to justice and nonviolence. They also shared their songs. Music, according to SNCC's Hollis Watkins, was part of all of their lives.

If we walked up to each other on the street or whatever, we would answer that with a song. "How did you wake up this morning?" [*singing in response*] "I woke up this morning with my mind stayed on freedom." Then other folks come up and they join in as a part of that. It was about where you were, what you were attempting to do.

The SNCC singers were young. Leaders were barely into their 20s. SNCC included high school students, too. These youths brought newer, secular songs to the cause. Says Watkins:

If you were dealing with a group of young folks, you want something that has a good tempo—you might start out with . . . "Calypso Freedom." When you do that, they fit right into it, they're in the groove with it.

"Calypso Freedom" put new words to Harry Belafonte's "Banana Boat" song. Here is one of the new verses:

*I took a little trip on the Greyhound bus*
*Freedom come and it won't be long*
*Just to fight segregation and this we must*
*Freedom come and it won't be long.*

Watkins was jailed in Parchman prison in Mississippi. He made up another verse, which he says is his own personal verse.

*If you don't believe that I've been to hell*
*Freedom come and it won't be long*
*Just follow me up to Parchman jail*
*Freedom come and it won't be long.*

But the young people also drew strength from the movement's religious songs. Bob Moses, another SNCC leader, wrote about another jail:

> We are smuggling this note from the drunk tank of the county jail in Magnolia, Mississippi. Twelve of us are here, sprawled out along the concrete bunker. . . .
>
> Later on, Hollis will lead out with a clear tenor into a freedom song, Talbert and Lewis will supply jokes, and McDew will discourse on the history of the black man and the Jew. McDew—a black by birth, a Jew by choice, and a revolutionary by necessity—has taken on the deep hates and deep loves which America and the world reserve for those who dare to stand in a strong sun and cast a sharp shadow . . .
>
> This is Mississippi, the middle of the iceberg. Hollis is leading off with his tenor, "Michael row the boat ashore, Alleluia; Christian brothers don't be slow, Alleluia; Mississippi's next to go, Alleluia." This is a tremor in the middle of the iceberg—from a stone that the builders rejected (from *SNCC: the New Abolitionists*, by Howard Zinn, p. 76).

Chuck McDew was the second chairperson of SNCC. He was black and Jewish. Even so, he preached and sang Christian gospel songs. "To me," he said, "they were movement songs." The gospel songs were "stuff that I'd heard all my life, but it didn't have much meaning. When I heard it down South, it had meaning."

"You had to be able to sing," insisted McDew. "You had to be able to preach. You had to be able to inspire. Music is very important in doing that. If you can't sing, you can't organize!"

As the civil rights movement of the 1960s grew, people from all parts of the country joined in. At first they did not know the gospel songs that were so familiar to black people, especially black church people. Soon, however, they felt the power of the music. They adopted the music of the movement, whether or not they shared its religious roots.

## Chapter 5

The Civil Rights Movement: The 1960s

*Black and white together*
*We shall not be moved*
*Just like a tree that's planted by the water*
*We shall not be moved.*

In many ways, the civil rights movement of the 1960s was a continuation of all that had gone before. Black people had been working for civil rights since slavery days. But some tactics of the movement changed in the 1960s. From lawsuits to demonstrations and marches, many more people took part in public actions. The violence of southern white resistance captured the attention of the world.

The Montgomery bus boycott was an important milestone in the civil rights movement. The bus boycott mobilized masses of people for legal, peaceful resistance.

In 1960, the focus moved to *civil disobedience*. The idea of civil disobedience was to deliberately and nonviolently break unjust segregation laws. By doing so, civil rights protesters hoped to focus public attention on the injustice. They hoped to force the government to change the laws. Of course it would take time for that to happen. Meanwhile, the protesters had to accept the consequences of breaking the law—arrest and jail.

On February 1, 1960, four black students bought school supplies in a Woolworth's store in Greensboro, North Carolina. Then they sat down at a lunch counter in the store. They were ready to eat. No one served them. Black people's money was welcome at Woolworth's stores in the South, but black people were not welcome to sit down at lunch counters. On that day, the four students sat at the lunch counter until the store closed.

*Sit-ins* focused on segregated lunch counters. Typically, an integrated group of students would sit down on the stools at a lunch counter. They tried to order coffee or a

On April 4, 1963, black college student Dorothy Bell of Birmingham, Alabama, waited in a downtown lunch counter for service that never came. Later that day, she was arrested with 20 others in sit-in attempts. *Associated Press*

1943. The restaurant had refused to serve black people, even though Chicago city law said this was illegal. The protesters won, but segregation continued. Other sit-ins took place in other cities over the next two decades. Between 1957 and 1960, at least 16 cities had seen sit-in protests. But it was the Greensboro sit-in that struck a spark. The students captured the imagination of young people across the nation. Similar protests began in other cities. The sit-in movement was launched.

The students who organized these sit-ins came from what are now called *historically black colleges*. These schools were founded to give black people a place to receive an education, at a time when most public and private colleges excluded them. Today, historically black colleges still nurture the strength and pride of black students. Fisk University, Spelman College, and Howard University are among the best known of more than 100 historically black colleges. Students from these colleges led the sit-in movement: John Lewis, James Bevel, Diane Nash, and many others became leaders in the civil rights movement.

hamburger. They were refused. They continued sitting. Sometimes white gangs attacked the students. They screamed insults and poured ketchup on the students' heads. They pulled students off the stools and beat them. Eventually, police would arrest the protesting students. They would charge the protesters with "trespass" or "disturbing the peace."

The first sit-in, organized by the Congress of Racial Equality, had been held at a Chicago lunch counter in

John Lewis grew up on a farm in Pike County, Alabama. With his brothers and sisters, he worked in the fields and picked cotton. Taking care of the family's flock of chickens, he learned responsibility before he was six years old. He also learned to love the chickens. He preached to the chickens, telling them to lead good lives and stop quarreling with one another. When a chicken died, John gave it a proper burial and preached a eulogy.

Music was woven through the life of the Lewis family. At night, they would gather around the radio and listen to music. Country music played during the week and gospel music on Sundays. Sundays brought live music, too. Local churches met only once a month. The Lewis family went to two churches so that they could have church more often. In his autobiography, John Lewis wrote:

> There were no hymnbooks in either church I attended as a child. Neither were there musical instruments. No piano. No organ. But there was music, music richer and fuller and sweeter than any I've heard since. I'm talking about pure singing, the sound of voices fueled by the spirit, people keeping rhythm with a beat they heard in their hearts, singing songs that came straight from their soul, with words they felt in every bone of their body.

In 1957, John Lewis left the farm for college. The American Baptist Theological Seminary in Nashville was small, with fewer than 100 students. It was conservative. The president did not want an NAACP chapter on campus. The college offered John Lewis a way to pay his costs by working in the kitchen. He seized the chance. He wanted to become a minister. He wanted to preach the gospel, but with a difference. He said preachers needed to focus less on heavenly streets of gold and more on what happened on the streets of Nashville.

John Lewis joined the Nashville Student Movement. This organization brought together students from several colleges. Together they studied the principles of nonviolence. Throughout 1959, they planned a sit-in movement. On Friday, February 12, 1960, the Nashville students were ready to launch their sit-ins. That night they sang and prayed together. One song stayed with John Lewis. It was a song that he would sing over and over during the coming years.

*I'm gonna do what the spirit says do*
*If the spirit says sit in, I'm gonna sit in*
*If the spirit says boycott, I'm gonna boycott*
*If the spirit says go to jail, I'm gonna go to jail*
*I'm gonna do what the spirit says do.*

The next morning, John Lewis put on his suit and tie. With 124 other young people, he marched down the street. John Lewis was now a movement leader. His 20th birthday was still a month ahead of him.

Newspapers and television news picked up the lunch counter sit-in stories. Quickly, the sit-in movement spread across the South. Black students or integrated groups sat in at lunch counters. They dressed in their best clothes. Sometimes they brought their books to study as they waited. They sat down and asked to be served. Stores refused. Students stayed.

The students followed the rules of nonviolence. In Nashville, the rules included:

Do show yourself friendly on the counter at all times.

Do sit straight and always face the counter.

Don't strike back, or curse back if attacked.

Don't laugh out.

Don't hold conversations.

Don't block entrances.

On February 27, 1960, a group of white teens attacked sit-in students in Nashville. The police let the white teens go, but arrested the sit-in students. They charged the students with "disorderly conduct" for sitting quietly at the counter. Z. Alexander Looby, a black lawyer, represented the students. On April 19, his house was bombed.

Neither arrests nor bombing stopped the students. They sat patiently as white people cursed them. They sat quietly as white people poured ketchup on their heads. They did not fight back when white people hit them, or knocked them off their chairs. Their courage made the

point. On May 10, Nashville lunch counters ended their policy of racial segregation.

Across the South, sit-ins continued. By the end of 1961, more than 3,000 people had been arrested in sit-ins.

## Students Organize in McComb, Mississippi

In 1961, some people thought Pike County was progressive. The rural Mississippi county had 250 registered black voters. Neighboring Amite and Walthall counties had not a single one.

Hollis Watkins grew up in rural Lincoln County, next door to Pike County. His parents were farmers, and he was the youngest of their 12 children. Hollis had gone to some NAACP meetings while he was in high school, but did not join. He explained:

At that time, most people, for example, who were members of the NAACP that were black did not let that be generally known. You have to know someone to get up close to them and they felt comfortable with you before they would let you know that they were members of the NAACP. People feared for their lives just for being members of the NAACP. So there was not a lot of political activities that was going on.

After high school, he was working on the family farm when he heard that Dr. Martin Luther King Jr. and "other big folks" were in McComb, a nearby city in Pike County. He and some friends went to check out the rumors.

Instead of well-known leaders, they found a young man from SNCC, Bob Moses. He explained that they were working on voter registration, and asked whether the four friends were interested in getting involved. Hollis joined SNCC and never looked back.

Throughout the summer of 1961, SNCC workers held voter registration classes in McComb. They met in McComb's Masonic Temple building. Some blacks in McComb succeeded in registering to vote. Then black people came from Amite County to ask for help. SNCC workers expanded their organizing efforts into the rural areas of Amite and Walthall counties. They met with resistance. Participants were arrested and beaten. Death threats multiplied.

SNCC's work continued into the fall. On September 25, 1961, SNCC workers in McComb got a phone call at the Masonic Temple. The call came from a doctor at a McComb funeral home. A body had been brought in. The body had been found in Liberty, a town in Amite County just 23 miles from McComb. Black and white people in the town of Liberty saw the body lying in the parking lot of a cotton gin. For hours, no one would touch the body. Finally, someone called the McComb funeral home to send a hearse. No one would tell who the dead man was. He had been shot in the head. The doctor

thought maybe the SNCC workers would know him. They did.

The dead man was Herbert Lee. He was a black farmer in Amite County. He had attended voter registration classes. He had been driving SNCC workers around the county. Now he had been shot to death—by E. H. Hurst, a member of the state legislature.

Hurst killed Herbert Lee in a public place in the middle of the morning. Witnesses were afraid to tell what happened. They knew they could be killed, too. Truth went underground. The murder was ruled "justifiable homicide." Hurst was not even arrested.

Despite the danger, young people in McComb seized the civil rights movement as their own. Jessie Nicholas was one of the young people. She recalled those days for the McComb Legacies project.

When I was about 12, some strangers came to town. . . . I wasn't allowed to talk to strangers. My mother told us that. But she never told me I couldn't follow them. When I saw Bob Moses [of SNCC], I followed him for about a week to see where he was going and what he was doing. But I never spoke to him, 'cause I wasn't allowed to. . . . I went back and gave my mother a full account and she told me I could talk to him. . . . I met him and we became friends. . . . My mother let us participate. . . .

You have to have certain principles in life. And you can't wait until you are 40 years old to develop those principles. And you have to stand up for yourself and know that you are right beyond the shadow of a doubt.

The McComb protests included attempts to integrate the public library, the Woolworth's lunch counter, and the Greyhound bus station.

Robert Talbert remembers:

Brenda Travis, myself, and Ike Lewis went to the train station in downtown McComb and didn't nothing happen. Then we got to the Woolworth. All the employees sat on the stools, so we couldn't sit there. Then we left there and went to the Greyhound bus station. After we went on the white side, the police came in and told us to leave. We didn't leave. He said it three times and then he arrested us.

Hollis Watkins talks about using singing in sit-ins:

At times when we were having sit-in demonstrations, they wouldn't serve us, would just ignore us. Maybe to prick the conscience of the owner of the restaurant, we would sing "I'm Gonna Sit at the Welcome Table." We would add verses that would hopefully prick the conscience of the owner. In addition to singing "I'm gonna tell God how you treat me," we would find out the name of the owner or the manager and would put that name in.

Sometimes when the police were standing there with dogs and sticks in hand, we'd sing, "I'm gonna tell God on Chief Larry in Greenwood, I'm gonna tell God on Chief Guy in McComb."

Hollis was arrested at the lunch counter. Before he turned 21, he was sent to jail. Jail was miserable. The young people were put in the "drunk tank."

"You had vomit, feces, and everything else all over the place," Watkins recalled years later. "There were no bunks and no beds, all we had was a . . . concrete slab. And in many cases, it was so nasty that you couldn't—you had to pick your spot even in terms of where to sit."

On October 3, 1961, the principal at Burglund High School, McComb's segregated black high school, expelled Brenda Travis. His reason: she had been arrested for participating in the sit-ins. Furious over the double injustice, about 300 students walked out of school. They marched to city hall and knelt in prayer on its steps. Some 116 students and three SNCC workers were arrested there. Their parents rallied behind the students. C. C. Bryant, the NAACP county president, had been skeptical of demonstrations. Now he declared, "Where the students lead, we will follow."

The students were jailed. After their release, they were expelled. A black junior college in Jackson, Mississippi, took in the students. Jackie Byrd was among those who went to Jackson for the rest of the school year after being expelled from Burglund High School for being arrested.

When the principal expelled students for demonstrating, high school students in McComb walked out. *McCain Library and Archives, University of Southern Mississippi*

SNCC held a Freedom School in McComb in 1961 and again in 1964. The schools taught people to read and write, and also taught about their rights. Freedom School education for young people and adults went hand in hand with voter registration efforts. The Ku Klux Klan bombed churches where meetings were held. They bombed homes where young civil rights workers stayed. They bombed the building that housed the Masonic Temple.

Finally, moderate white citizens in McComb had had enough. More than 600 signed a "Statement of Principles" denouncing the violence. The known bombers were arrested, though they were not sent to prison. But the violence in McComb ended.

## Freedom Rides

In the spring of 1961, another group of activists gathered in Washington. Some were members of CORE. Some were members of SNCC. They were young and old, black and white. They planned to challenge segregation by riding Greyhound and Trailways buses through the South.

The first group set out in May. Some white passengers sat in the back of the bus, some black passengers sat in the front. The integrated group ignored the "white" and "colored" signs on restrooms and waiting rooms.

On May 5, the violence began. The bus stopped at Rock Hill, South Carolina. John Lewis, a 21-year-old SNCC student, walked toward the "white" waiting room. Two young white men stepped in front of him. They told him to go to the "colored" entrance.

Lewis refused. "I have a right to go in here on grounds of the Supreme Court decision in the *Boynton* case," he said.

When the Freedom Riders headed South, segregation was *already* illegal. Segregation in interstate buses had been ruled illegal decades earlier. The U.S. Supreme Court decided the case of *Boynton v. Virginia* in December 1960. The Boynton decision said that segregation also was illegal in all waiting rooms and restaurants serving interstate bus passengers. The Freedom Riders were not protesting the law. They were following the law. They asked that the law be enforced.

The white men attacked, beating John Lewis, Albert Bigelow, and Genevieve Hughes to the ground. Bigelow was a Harvard-educated former Navy captain. Genevieve Hughes was a 28-year-old white stockbroker from New York. Police stopped the attack, and the ride continued.

As the buses went farther south, the violence grew. One bus was burned, its passengers barely escaping. Riders were badly beaten. Some suffered permanent injuries. State officials jailed Freedom Riders. They ignored the crimes of the white mobs. Some mobs also attacked reporters. That brought more media attention.

John Lewis wrote about the Freedom Rides, and about the songs that accompanied the riders. "Freedom songs," he wrote in his autobiography. "Songs of the movement. The songs we'd been singing for years now and would keep singing for years to come." The songs kept up their spirits as they sat, locked into a bus in Birmingham. Remembering the beatings endured by fellow riders and the bombing of another bus, they sang on the bus. Hours later, they sang in the jail. They sang for themselves, their songs bridging the bars and corridors separating black from white and men from women. They sang because they knew their singing was "one of the worst things" for police commissioner Bull Connor and the jail guards.

Out of jail in Birmingham, they got back on a bus headed to Jackson, Mississippi.

*I'm taking a ride on the Greyhound bus line*
*I'm riding the front seat to Jackson this time*
*Hallelujah, I'm a-traveling*
*Hallelujah, ain't it fine*
*Hallelujah, I'm a-traveling*
*Down freedom's main line.*

Arriving in Jackson, they were arrested again. By now, hundreds of northern freedom riders were taking buses south. Jails overflowed with civil rights protesters. Lewis and others ended up at the Parchman state penitentiary.

Bombs and violence kept the first group of Freedom Riders from completing their ride. Then a group of Nashville students took up the cause. As each group was stopped, another took its place. More than 400 people joined the Freedom Rides at some time during the summer.

## The Birmingham Campaign

In 1963, Dr. Martin Luther King Jr. went to Birmingham. He and the Southern Christian Leadership Conference launched a campaign in the Alabama city. Their targets included segregated stores and lunch counters. They also wanted jobs for black people.

The 16th Street Baptist Church in Birmingham was a major gathering place for the campaign. Like all southern churches (and most northern churches), 16th Street Baptist was a one-race church. It was a black church, with

Young nonviolent warriors under arrest in Birmingham. Policemen are leading a group of black school children into jail, following their arrest for protesting against racial discrimination near the city hall of Birmingham, Alabama, on May 4, 1963. *Bill Hudson, Associated Press*

very violent police force, led by Commissioner Bull Connor. April saw lunch-counter sit-ins and marches on city hall. Some people were arrested and jailed. Bull Connor promised to fill the jails with black protesters. The press and the nation paid little attention.

Teenagers and children wanted to march for freedom. They wanted to take their places in the movement. Their parents were afraid. They knew what could happen to black youth who "got out of line." They knew about clubs and tear gas and jails. They knew about beatings and lynchings. They feared for their children's safety. Parents resisted, but children insisted.

black ministers and black members. It had been founded in 1873 by former slaves. Back then it was called the First Colored Baptist Church of Birmingham. The current church building had been designed in 1909 by the first black architect in Alabama. Prominent black Americans like Booker T. Washington, W. E. B. Dubois, Marian Anderson, and Paul Robeson had all come to this church in their day, to preach or to teach, to pray or to sing.

As the 1963 campaign proceeded, Birmingham quickly became a battleground. On one side were the nonviolent civil rights workers. On the other side was the

Young leaders from the Student Nonviolent Coordinating Committee pushed for greater involvement by college and high school students. The Reverend James Bevel told young people to follow their consciences. He knew that parents disapproved. But, he said, even "against your Mama, you have a right to make this witness."

On May 2, children filled the churches. Then they flowed out into the streets of Birmingham. Police arrested high school students and even younger protesters. The youngest person arrested was six years old. In all, 600 children were crammed into Birmingham jails by nightfall.

★ ★ ★ ★ ★

## Letter from a Birmingham Jail

Dr. Martin Luther King Jr. went to jail in Birmingham for nine days. From jail, he wrote an impassioned letter to white ministers who had criticized his actions and advised black people to be patient and wait. "I guess it is easy for those who have never felt the stinging darts of segregation to say, 'Wait,'" he wrote. "But when you have seen vicious mobs lynch your mothers and fathers at will . . . when you have seen hate-filled policemen curse, kick, brutalize and even kill your black brothers and sisters with impunity; when you see the vast majority of your

twenty million Negro brothers smothering in an air-tight cage of poverty in the midst of an affluent society; . . . when you are humiliated day in and day out by nagging signs reading 'white' and 'colored'; when your first name becomes 'nigger' and your middle name becomes 'boy' (however old you are) . . . then you will understand why we find it difficult to wait."

★ ★ ★ ★ ★

The next day, more young people filled the streets, marching and singing. Police turned fire hoses on the young marchers, sending them tumbling along the ground. Bull Connor turned police dogs on them, too. Now the press paid attention. Television cameras and reporters focused the eyes of the nation and world on Birmingham.

Parents followed their children into the churches and streets. For weeks, singing and speeches filled the churches at night. Determined nonviolent demonstrators filled first the streets and then the jails. In 38 days, more than 2,500 people were arrested. Two thousand of them were children.

The city's business leaders grew more and more unhappy. Between marches and boycotts, they were losing money. Finally, they gave in. They agreed to end segregation in downtown stores. They also agreed to hire black workers.

Victory seemed to bring more violence. An outraged Ku Klux Klan led the way. The Klan bombed the homes

Dr. Martin Luther King Jr., left, was jailed for protesting segregation in Birmingham. His powerful "Letter from a Birmingham Jail" explained the reasons for nonviolent civil disobedience. *Horace Cort, Associated Press*

of civil rights leaders. By September, Birmingham had seen 20-plus bombings, all unsolved. They earned it the nickname of "Bombingham."

Federal courts already had ordered Birmingham schools to let black children in. Alabama Governor George Wallace said no. He sent National Guard troops to prevent black children from attending "white" schools. President John F. Kennedy ordered the National Guard troops to withdraw.

Birmingham was at war with itself. Many white students boycotted the schools. Some white cheerleaders and football players at West End High organized to support integration. Crowds of white students and parents marched at the schools. They threw rocks to keep black students out.

## Birmingham Sunday

In the middle of September's madness, the 16th Street Baptist Church celebrated its annual Youth Day. In 1963, people got dressed up in their Sunday best to go to church. North and South, black and white, men and boys wore suits and ties to church. Women and girls wore hats and white gloves. Dressing up was a way to show respect—and it was fun, too. People enjoyed looking good as they gathered with their friends at church.

On Youth Day, September 15, 1963, the children of 16th Street Baptist Church were looking especially good. Because it was Youth Day, some of the teens would lead the

Demonstrators were sprayed with fire hoses in Birmingham, sending them tumbling down the street. *Bill Hudson, Associated Press*

service. The girls dressed in white. As usual, they came for Sunday school, held in the basement before services. Four girls left their class a little early. In front of the bathroom mirror, they combed their hair one last time before services. Happy and excited, they wanted to look their best as they stood in front of the congregation, in front of their parents and relatives and neighbors and friends.

Addie Mae Collins was 14 years old, the seventh of eight children in her family. Her father was a janitor. Her mother stayed at home with the children and sewed potholders and aprons. Addie and her sister sold the potholders and aprons door-to-door. Addie liked to draw, especially portraits of people. She also liked to pitch in softball games. She was a peacemaker among her sisters and brothers. Addie Mae was in eighth grade at Hill Elementary School.

In Birmingham, police set dogs on demonstrators. This photo shows a dog attacking a 17-year-old. *Bill Hudson, Associated Press*

Carole Robertson, also 14, was the youngest of three children. Her father was a band teacher and her mother a librarian. Carole was a star. She belonged to a marching band at Parker High School, to the school science club, to the Girl Scouts, and to other organizations. She was a straight-A student, who also danced, played the clarinet, and sang.

Cynthia Wesley, another 14-year-old, was the adopted child of schoolteacher parents. Her father was the principal of Lewis Elementary School. She attended Ullman High School, and often invited friends to backyard parties at her house.

Carol Denise McNair, called "Niecie" by her friends, was the only child of a photo shop owner and a teacher. She was only 11 years old. She wanted to become a doctor. She staged talent shows in her neighborhood every year to raise money for muscular dystrophy research. She

also held tea parties and played baseball. And she believed she should be able to eat at the same lunch counter with white children.

Addie Mae's little sister, Sarah, was with the four older girls. As she stood at the sink washing her hands, she watched them standing next to the basement window. She saw Addie Mae fixing Denise's sash.

And then, at 10:22 A.M., 19 sticks of dynamite blasted her world away. Blinded by shrapnel, Sarah staggered out of the room. Addie Mae and Niecie and Carole and Cynthia were gone forever. Sarah suffered through many operations. Though she lost her right eye, Sarah would see again. She was one of more than 20 people injured in the bombing.

The church bombing, and the deaths of four innocent children, shook the nation. In Birmingham, white strangers came to the door of the McNair home that afternoon to say how sorry they were. Charles Morgan, a white Birmingham attorney, declared that all whites were guilty of the bombing, saying, "We all did it." On September 18, 800 black and white pastors were among the masses of people gathered for the funeral of three of the girls. (Carole Robertson had a separate funeral.)

Even this horrendous event did not touch the deep racism of many white residents of Birmingham. On the very afternoon of September 15, two white Eagle Scouts were headed home from a segregationist rally. The hate-filled speeches of the rally stayed with them. They saw a 13-year-old black boy, Virgil Ware, riding with his friend

Lakeyah Scales participated in the Chicago Children's Choir's Freedom Tour in 2007. She was about to begin her junior year at Queen of Peace High School in a Chicago suburb. This was Lakeyah's ninth year as a member of the choir. In previous years, she had gone on choir tours to Pennsylvania, Maine, Alabama, Massachusetts, and even Japan. "Of all my tours," Lakeyah said at the beginning, "this will be the most impactful."

Lakeyah's great-great-grandfather was a slave before the Civil War. Her grandmother and aunts and uncles live in Birmingham. They lived in Birmingham during the 1960s. She had never talked to them about the 1950s and 1960s. She did not know their stories. They had never talked with her about the civil rights movement.

Lakeyah's mother, Monica Scales, said, "My mother talked about how hard the times were, how segregated the schools were. She was in the midst of some of the activities around the marches. I'm not sure if she actually marched. There were meetings and rallies—she was at those."

Monica Scales said she shielded her children from painful family stories of living in the South before the movement. Still, she worries that young people "don't get a real sense of that history from the school." She believes that the Freedom Tour gave the CCC members the exposure they needed. To her, the CCC is "an awesome group of kids.

They are bringing people together of all backgrounds and nationalities."

Lakeyah's Birmingham family came to the 16th Street Baptist Church in Montgomery, Alabama, to hear her sing. As the tour went on, she talked to her mother about what she was learning. She told her mother that the tour was a life-changing event.

Lakeyah Scales singing after marching across the Edmund Pettus Bridge in Selma in 2007. *Mary C. Turck*

**"Of all my tours, this will be the most impactful."**

on a bicycle. The two Scouts shot and killed him. They told police they didn't know why they shot him.

Battles broke out in Birmingham streets that Sunday. Mostly young people fought. Black and white teens threw rocks at one another. Police broke up the fights. Of course, they took the side of the white fighters. A young black man, 16-year-old Johnny Robinson, fled. Police shot him in the back of the head, killing him.

Pain that ran so deep came out in poetry and preaching and song. Dudley Randall, a 49-year-old African American poet and librarian, wrote "Ballad of Birmingham." His poem tells of a young girl asking her mother to let her march for freedom. Her mother says no, "For the dogs are fierce and wild, / And clubs and hoses, guns and jails / Aren't good for a little child." Instead, the mother sends her daughter to church. In the poem, the daughter is then killed by a bomb. Randall later established Broadside Press, which published African American poetry and literary essays. Folksinger Richard Farina also was moved to write about that terrible day, in the song "Birmingham Sunday." (It's on the Chicago Children's Choir CD, *Songs on the Road to Freedom*, which accompanies this book.)

## Birmingham Sunday

Copyright 1964 by Richard Farina

*Come round by my side and I'll sing you a song*
*I'll sing it so softly, it'll do no one wrong*

*On Birmingham Sunday the blood ran like wine*
*And the choirs kept singing of Freedom.*

*That cold autumn morning no eyes saw the sun*
*And Addie Mae Collins, her number was one*
*At an old Baptist church there was no need to run*
*And the choirs kept singing of Freedom.*

*The clouds they were gray and the autumn winds blew*
*And Denise McNair brought the number to two*
*The falcon of death was a creature they knew*
*And the choirs kept singing of Freedom.*

*The church it was crowded, but no one could see*
*That Cynthia Wesley's dark number was three*
*Her prayers and her feelings would shame you and me*
*And the choirs kept singing of Freedom.*

*Young Carol Robertson entered the door*
*And the number her killers had given was four*
*She asked for a blessing but asked for no more*
*And the choirs kept singing of Freedom.*

*On Birmingham Sunday a noise shook the ground*
*And people all over the earth turned around*
*For no one recalled a more cowardly sound*
*And the choirs kept singing of Freedom.*

*The men in the forest they once asked of me*
*How many black berries grew in the Blue Sea*

*And I asked them right with a tear in my eye*
*How many dark ships in the forest?*

*The Sunday has come and the Sunday has gone*
*And I can't do much more than to sing you a song*
*I'll sing it so softly, it'll do no one wrong*
*And the choirs keep singing of Freedom.*

The Federal Bureau of Investigation was supposed to investigate the church bombing. The FBI was responsible for investigating civil rights violations. In this case, and in many others, it dragged its feet in the investigation. The church bombing was in 1963. No one was taken to court for 14 years! Finally, in 1977, Robert "Dynamite Bob" Chambliss was convicted. In 2001, former Ku Klux Klan member Thomas Blanton also was convicted of the bombing and sentenced to life in prison.

Birmingham Sunday marked a milestone in the movement. The sad milestone was only one of many. The list of martyrs had begun years before. The killing continued long after Birmingham Sunday.

## Educating, Organizing, Moving On

Sit-ins, marches, and demonstrations got a lot of attention. Other civil rights work went on more quietly.

Septima Clark was a black teacher in South Carolina. She fought for equal pay for black teachers. She was fired

because she was a member of the NAACP. Then she started *Citizenship Schools*. Citizenship Schools taught black adults to read. They needed to read so that they could register to vote.

Clark went to work at the Highlander Center. Her Citizenship Schools spread across the South. Whites harassed the schools and their teachers and students. The Citizenship Schools still kept going.

"There were 897 [schools] going from 1957 to 1970," Septima recalled years later. "They were in people's kitchens, in beauty parlors, and under trees in the summertime. I went all over the South, sometimes visiting three Citizenship Schools in one day, checking to be sure they were teaching people to read those election laws and to write their names in cursive writing."

From one place to another, the movement took different shapes. In some places, schools were the focus. In others, organizers focused on voting. Sit-ins spread to movie theaters and public libraries. People staged "wade-ins" at public swimming pools and beaches. In Florida, protesters tried to integrate churches.

People suffered for the movement. In Mississippi, Annell Ponder and Fannie Lou Hamer were jailed. Both women were beaten, over and over again. They carried the injuries for the rest of their lives.

Medgar Evers headed the NAACP in Mississippi. He and his wife had three small children. They lived in Jackson, Mississippi. Medgar and Myrlie Evers knew how dan-

# Voices of the Choir

History classes teach relatively little about the civil rights movement. "At school, we only learn about Martin Luther King Jr., Malcolm X, and Rosa Parks," Stephanie Ricoy says. "That's it. That's black history and the civil rights movement. The white history changes year to year, but black history month is always the same. I didn't know about the fifth child who was killed on Birmingham Sunday [Virgil Ware] until we came here."

Julia Henderson agrees. "Being here, where it all happened, I am learning so much more. So much more happened than what they tell us in school."

"They don't give you any idea," Stephanie adds, "and a half truth equals a whole lie."

Julia Henderson and Stephanie Ricoy. *Mary C. Turck*

**"I am learning so much more. So much more happened than what they tell us in school."**

gerous his job was. Frequent death threats reminded them. Committed to the movement, they did not back down.

On June 11, 1963, Medgar Evers returned home late, after a meeting. He got out of his car in front of his home. A Ku Klux Klansman waited in the bushes. He shot Medgar Evers. The bullet went through his body and through the living room window into his home. Evers was pronounced dead at the hospital less than an hour later.

Throughout those bloody years, the world's attention focused on the civil rights movement in the United States. The movement spread across the South, and so did its songs.

Chuck McDew described SNCC's special songs:

The Freedom Song was so old and so much a part of the history of the struggle in this country that, back in slavery days, you'd have your tongue cut out for singing it. And it was forbidden to be sung—you couldn't sing it in churches. It was in those dark places hidden from the public eye where you could sing it.

So when it was first sung publicly was when the Union Army came down through Georgia. . . . It was always the anthem of the movement and the striving for freedom.

**Oh, Freedom (The Freedom Song)**

(Traditional)

*Oh, freedom*
*Oh, freedom*

*Oh, freedom*
*Over me*
*And before I'll be a slave*
*I'll be buried in my grave*
*And go home to my Lord and be free.*

*No segregation*
*No segregation*
*No more segregation*
*Over me*
*And before I'll be a slave*
*I'll be buried in my grave*
*And go home to my Lord and be free.*

*No more weepin'*
*No more weepin'*
*No more weepin'*
*Over me*
*And before I'll be a slave*
*I'll be buried in my grave*
*And go home to my Lord and be free.*

We felt that it was the clearest sort of expression of that hope, not hidden like words in spirituals and stuff like that. You didn't have to figure it out—everybody knew when you sang: "Oh, freedom—before I'll be a slave, I'll be buried in my grave and go home to my God and be free."

With SNCC we sang it all the time. That song was an expression of hope, even more so than "We Shall Overcome." There were two—that song, "Oh, Freedom"—and

"This May Be the Last Time"—that were songs that were particularly SNCC songs. Everybody knows "We Shall Overcome." All the meetings, you'd finish with "We Shall Overcome." In SNCC meetings, the song we always would start meetings with was "Oh, Freedom," and we'd finish the meetings with "This May Be the Last Time."

And it was particularly important. Every time I even hear it, I see people in my mind's eye. We would stand in a circle and hold hands and sing "This May Be the Last Time." I can see in my mind's eye people whose hands I was holding or whose eyes I was looking at where it was the last time I ever saw them on this earth. And that was like saying good-bye every time we closed the meeting. It was like understanding you may never, ever again in life see the person that you are looking at right now. That song goes way back. It was the song people would sing when they were going to attempt to escape from slavery. It had such meaning because even if people did escape, more than likely you never saw them again. You would spend time wondering whether or not so-and-so ever made it or if they were killed along the way. You'd remember that just before you left on your journey—you held hands and sang "This May Be the Last Time."

**This May Be the Last Time**
(Traditional)

*This may be the last time*
*This may be the last time, children*

*This may be the last time*
*May be the last time, children, I don't know*
*May be the last time we all stand together*
*May be the last time, I don't know*
*May be the last time we all sing together*
*May be the last time, I don't know.*

## Taking the Movement National

Marches and demonstrations in the South would not be enough. To win the battle for justice, the nation needed new laws. These laws had to come from Washington.

A march on Washington had been planned in 1941. A. Philip Randolph was a black union leader. He planned a march to demand jobs for black people. President Franklin Roosevelt responded to the plans. He issued an executive order to ban discrimination in defense industries.

In 1962, Randolph began planning a new march. He met with long-time activist Bayard Rustin, who took the lead in organizing the march. They talked about a march for civil rights and economic justice. They knew a coalition would be needed. Martin Luther King Jr. agreed to join in the planning. Other civil rights organizations also joined in.

The March on Washington was a huge news event. Many people were afraid it would cause violence. They did not believe that so many black people would protest peacefully. Many police were called out to protect the city from the marchers.

Not even the organizers expected the huge crowd that came. Buses poured into Washington from all over the nation. Many white people joined in the march. Hundreds of thousands of people assembled at the Washington Monument under a blazing August sun. Throughout the morning a series of entertainers sang for and with them. Famous musicians (see chapter 6) and the SNCC Freedom Singers took turns on stage. Then the crowd marched to the Lincoln Memorial. There they heard the scheduled speakers—and more songs.

John Lewis was the youngest speaker. He spoke about living in fear. He called on people to recognize "that we are involved in a serious social revolution." He denounced politicians who "build their careers on immoral compromises and ally themselves with open forms of political, economic, and social exploitation." Lewis was the only speaker to use the words "black people" instead of "Negroes." (In 1987, he was elected to the U.S. Congress. Ever since he has represented the Fifth U.S. Congressional District of Georgia.)

Dr. Martin Luther King Jr. spoke last. He preached a sermon to the country. "I have a dream," he told the nation. His dream was "deeply rooted in the American dream." He spoke of a dream that "my four little children will one day live in a nation where they will not be judged by the color of their skin but by the content of their character." He ended with a quotation from a song:

And when this happens, when we allow freedom to ring, when we let it ring from every village and every hamlet, from every state and every city, we will be able to speed up that day when all of God's children, black men and white men, Jews and Gentiles, Protestants and Catholics, will be able to join hands and sing in the words of the old Negro spiritual, "Free at last, free at last. Thank God Almighty, we are free at last."

And at the end, the great march closed with another song. Mahalia Jackson led the crowd in "We Shall Overcome." The demonstration had been peaceful and dignified. From singing to speeches, the point was made: Black people had waited too long for justice. It was time for Congress to act.

It was less than a month after the march that the four girls died in the Birmingham church bombing. Then, at the end of 1963, President John F. Kennedy was assassinated.

A grieving nation wanted to make amends. President Kennedy had endorsed the civil rights act. The new president, Lyndon Baines Johnson, insisted that it was needed. He twisted arms in Congress. He made deals. He spoke out for civil rights. Finally, Congress passed the new law.

The 1964 Civil Rights Act outlawed discrimination in employment and public accommodations. The term *public accommodations* included most restaurants, movie theaters, stores, and other businesses. The new law prohibited state governments from denying access to public facilities on the grounds of race. The law gave the attorney general more power to desegregate schools. Discrimination in employment was outlawed.

# Freedom Summer

In 1964, hundreds of volunteers swept south for Freedom Summer. Their mission was to register black voters.

Southern states used poll taxes and literacy tests to keep black people from voting. A poll tax meant people had to pay to register to vote. Poor people could not afford to pay the poll tax, and most black people were poor.

Literacy tests also kept black people from registering. Local officials let white people register without testing, but they set high standards for black people. Sometimes they asked black people to recite part of the U.S. Constitution. Sometimes they asked them to explain a part of the Constitution. Local officials decided who passed and who did not. They almost never let black people pass.

Violence also prevented voter registration. Black people who tried to register were threatened. Some were killed. Their murders warned others to stay away from voting.

Freedom Summer began with murder. Three young volunteers were arrested in Mississippi and released at night to be followed and killed by waiting Klansmen.

James Chaney was a 21-year-old black man from Meridian, Mississippi. His involvement in the civil rights movement began while he was still in high school, and continued through the years. He had joined CORE in 1963, and worked on Freedom Summer preparations during 1964. He had gone to Ohio to help train the college students, and returned with Michael Schwerner.

Michael and Rita Schwerner had come to Mississippi in January to prepare for Freedom Summer. They, too, had been in Ohio, training the northern college student volunteers, until June 21. That Sunday, Michael headed back to Mississippi with a station wagon full of volunteers. Rita remained behind in Ohio, working on training volunteers.

Andrew Goodman was a 20-year-old anthropology student from New York. He had come to Ohio as one of the college student volunteers.

The bodies of the three young volunteers were hidden by their murderers. They were not found until August. No one was convicted of the murders until 2005. Even then, only a single person was convicted.

The murders focused attention on Mississippi, but they did not stop Freedom Summer. McComb, Mississippi, was one of the Freedom Summer towns. The violence in McComb shows what happened when black Mississippians tried to register to vote.

In McComb, the SNCC Freedom House was bombed on July 8. Two workers were injured.

Bombs could not stop the movement. By July 15, McComb's Freedom School had 35 students. The school was held in St. Mary's Church in McComb. St. Mary's pastor had another church, Mount Zion Hill Baptist, in rural Pike County. On July 17, Mount Zion Hill Baptist Church was burned to the ground.

The Freedom School kept on. By July 21, enrollment reached 75. On July 22, Mount Vernon Missionary Baptist church was burned. The church had not been involved in Freedom Summer, but it was a black church. So was Rose Hill Church in neighboring Amite County. Rose Hill Church was burned on the night of July 23/24.

Throughout the summer, the violence continued, not only in McComb but across the state.

Ben Chaney was 10 years old when his brother, James Chaney, was murdered. In a 1999 speech, Ben Chaney said:

> In Mississippi, in the 1960s, when segregation was king, racism the status quo, and bigotry the law, it was young people who rose up and challenged the system. In racially segregated and economically depressed Neshoba County, Mississippi, it was the local black youth and northern volunteers who challenged racism and led the fight for freedom and justice. Because of the sacrifices made by many people, most of the obvious signs of racism and bigotry have been eliminated.

# Bloody Sunday and the Selma March

In 1965, Sheyann Webb was eight years old. She lived in Selma, Alabama. One day, she noticed black and white

people talking together in front of Brown Chapel African Methodist Episcopal Church. That made her curious. What could be going on? Black and white people didn't associate with each other. Even at eight years old, Sheyann knew that.

Sheyann followed the people inside the church. She listened and tried to understand what was happening. She heard that Dr. Martin Luther King Jr. was coming to town. She heard about voter registration and civil rights. She liked what she heard.

Sheyann went home and asked her parents some questions. Were they registered to vote? Her mother explained that they were not, and that if they registered, they would be fired from their jobs. Then they would not have money to feed the family.

Sheyann began going to the church meetings. She liked the meetings and the singing and clapping. She liked the talk about civil rights. She even met Dr. King.

Her parents told her not to go to the meetings. They were afraid of what might happen. She kept on going anyway. At first, her teachers did not go to the meetings. They were afraid of losing their jobs. But they would ask Sheyann what happened at the meetings. Later, 100 black schoolteachers marched. They demanded the right to vote.

As the campaign continued, violence grew. On February 18, police attacked demonstrators. Some ran into a café, trying to escape the police. Police followed and continued beating them. Jimmie Lee Jackson tried to protect his mother and 82-year-old grandfather from the beatings. State police shot him. He died eight days later.

The black community was outraged and frightened. Protesters planned a march from Selma to the state capital in Montgomery. The march was set for Sunday, March 7.

Sheyann went to the meeting the night before the march. In an interview years later, she remembered feeling frightened but determined. "I couldn't really sleep well," she said. "After I had come home from that meeting, I asked my mother, would she march, and I told her that I was going to march anyway, and she did tell me, if I marched I will be whipped." Sheyann went anyway.

> I remember walking, and as we got closer and closer to the [Edmund Pettus Bridge], my eyes began to water, that's just how afraid I was. And I wanted to turn back and I didn't want to turn back. And I said to myself, if they can go, I can go, too. And I remember as we approached the bridge, I was getting frightened more and more and as we got to the top of the bridge, I could see hundreds of policemen, state troopers, billy clubs, dogs, and horses, and I began to just cry.

The ministers at the front of the march knelt to pray, and so did Sheyann.

> I knelt down and I said to myself, Lord, help me. And once we had gotten up, all I could remember was outbursts of tear gas, and I saw people being beaten, and I began to

just try to run home as fast as I could. And as I began to run home, I saw horses behind me, and I will never forget a Freedom Fighter picked me up, Hosea Williams, and I told him to put me down—he wasn't running fast enough. And I ran, and I ran, and I ran. It was like I was running for my life. . . . But I did it . . . and I was willing to go again, and that night I wrote my funeral arrangements.

Dr. Martin Luther King Jr. led a second march two days later. This march turned back when confronted by police. That night, three white ministers who had come to march ate dinner at a black café. As they left, a white mob attacked them. They clubbed the Reverend James Reeb into unconsciousness. He died two days later.

An outraged nation watched Selma on television. President Lyndon Johnson sent federal troops to protect the marchers. On March 21, the marchers set out again. Sheyann walked with them. Once again, she marched without her parents' permission. She left a note on the washing machine telling them that she had gone to march.

Five days later, 22,000 marchers arrived in Montgomery. Sheyann's parents were there to take her home. She was suspended from school, but she did not get the whipping that she feared.

This march had been peaceful, but the killing continued. Viola Liuzzo had come from Detroit to march. Afterward, she drove marchers back to Selma. On the highway, Ku Klux Klansmen drove alongside her car. They saw a white woman driving and black men in the car. They shot Viola Liuzzo in the face, killing her. ("Murder on the Road in Alabama," one of the songs on the CD *Songs on the Road to Freedom*, is about the killing of Viola Liuzzo.)

Sheyann asked her parents to register to vote, as a birthday present to her. They did. They took her along with them to the polls when they voted.

In 1965, Congress passed the Voting Rights Act. This law outlawed poll taxes and literacy tests. It also gave the federal government power to protect voting rights.

Laws are not enough. To make the laws work, people must act. They must claim the rights guaranteed under law. Throughout the 1960s, the movement continued, marching to the drumbeat of freedom.

## Chicago Children's Choir at Selma

Today Selma is home to the Slavery Museum and the National Voting Rights Museum. Joanne Bland is the director of the National Voting Rights Museum. She was 11 years old on Bloody Sunday, and, like Sheyann, she marched that day.

The Chicago Children's Choir came to Selma during their Freedom Tour 2007. They visited both museums. Then Joanne Bland took them to the Edmund Pettus Bridge. She led them across the bridge, retracing the route of the original march. No singing was scheduled, but the choir could not stop. Nothing but singing could express their emotions as they marched across the

bridge and then drove on to Montgomery.

In Montgomery, they visited the Rosa Parks Museum, Dr. King's church, just down the street from the state capitol, and the Civil Rights Memorial.

"I couldn't have asked for more than what I've gotten," choir member Jasmine Henderson reflected. "To know that I've some-what been exposed to my own history in a textbook is very important to me, but to see it with my own eyes makes everything come alive for me. . . . I am truly grateful for everything that my elders have done for me to get me to the point where I am."

Chapter 6

Jazzing Up the Melody of a Movement

*Come mothers and fathers throughout the land*
*And don't criticize what you can't understand . . .*
*For the times they are a-changin'.*

Just as the times change, so does the music of the times. African American music had strong roots in spirituals and gospel songs. This was Christian religious music. Religious people sang it in church and at home. Religious singers recorded it and sang it on the radio. As good church people, they stayed away from nightclubs.

Other African American musicians performed outside the churches. They played and sang blues and jazz. They developed folk music, rock 'n' roll, soul music, and rhythm and blues. This was secular music, nonreligious and not welcome in the churches.

Many church people thought that secular music was sinful. They would not go near nightclubs, because drinking was also sinful. Some would not listen to secular music on the radio. A "good" churchgoer would only sing religious music. A "good" gospel music performer would not sing the blues.

Most of the leaders of the 20th century civil rights movement had deep religious roots. Many were ministers—Dr. Martin Luther King Jr., Reverend Ralph Abernathy, Reverend C. T. Vivien, and later, Reverend Jesse Jackson among them. Many of the students who started the Student Nonviolent Coordinating Committee were studying to become ministers. The meetings for the movement were held in churches, not in nightclubs.

As the civil rights movement grew, its leaders recognized that non-Christian and nonreligious people were also giving their lives to the movement. Nonbelievers came inside the churches for mass meetings. Baptists sat in mass meetings side by side with Catholics, Jews, and nonbelievers. As people sang and marched and went to jail together, the old walls between them came down.

For decades, musicians had broken through the wall between secular and sacred music. Secular musicians had given voice to the message of the movement. They sang the movement in many different melodies. Their music reached people who stayed outside the churches and outside Christian religious groups.

The roots of secular civil rights music go back to the jazz and blues of the early 20th century.

## The Great Migration and the Harlem Renaissance

Between the beginning of World War I in 1914 and the Great Depression of the 1930s, black people moved from South to North. Millions left the rural South for urban centers, especially New York, Detroit, and Chicago. This movement is called the *Great Migration*. It was driven both by a desire to escape oppression and by the prospect of jobs and a better life in the North.

As more black people settled in the North, black culture blossomed. In New York City, Harlem was the neighborhood where most black people settled. There, black poets, writers, actors, and musicians found places to tell their stories and make their music. They sparked an artistic and intellectual movement. This creative outpouring was called the *Harlem Renaissance*.

A leading figure in the Harlem Renaissance was Paul Robeson. His father was a runaway slave. Robeson became an actor, an athlete, a lawyer, a singer, and a political activist. Though he was better known as an actor and activist, Robeson's powerful voice moved concert audiences in New York to London. His best-known song is probably "Ol' Man River," from the 1927 musical *Show Boat*. He changed the words of one line of the song from "I'm tired of living and scared of dying" to "I'll keep on fighting until I'm dying."

Along with black musicians, new forms of black music flourished in the Harlem Renaissance. Black and white people mingled in Harlem nightclubs to hear *jazz* and *blues*.

## Jazz and Blues

Jazz and blues have deep roots in the African American experience. Blues songs echo some of the songs of slavery days. Jazz appeared in the early 20th century. Jazz was known as black music. This led some to condemn jazz.

"Jazz is often associated with vile surroundings, filthy words, unmentionable dances," said one U.S. editor. In Germany, the Nazis barred both black foreigners and jazz—which they called "Nigger-Jew Music."

In the early days most jazz and blues musicians were black. Many still are. Most recording companies, nightclubs, and concert halls were white-owned in the 1950s and 1960s. Black musicians performed in hotels that would not let them stay in a room. They played in nightclubs where they would not be welcome in the audience. Sometimes they also integrated clubs. They broke through some race barriers. Many staunchly supported the civil rights movement.

# Billie Holiday

Billie Holiday's life was a blues story. Born to a 13-year-old mother, she had a difficult childhood. Her early teenage years included time in reform school. She was raped by a neighbor.

As an adult, Billie Holiday suffered from drug addiction. She served time in prison for drug use. Men in her life abused her.

After her difficult early life, her career began in Harlem's jazz clubs in the 1930s. Her incredible voice brought her fame. Despite her personal pain, she succeeded as a singer. She toured Europe and performed in Carnegie Hall. She died in 1959 at the age of 44.

In the 1930s, Billie Holiday encountered a song about lynching. "Strange Fruit" had been written by a Jewish schoolteacher from the Bronx, Abel Meeropol. He wrote it as a poem, under the pseudonym Lewis Allen. The poem marked the lynching of two young black men in the 1930s. The song referred to the "strange fruit" on southern trees—the bodies of lynched black men. His poem was set to music.

Billie Holiday was deeply moved by the song. She made "Strange Fruit" her signature song. It soon became a Billie Holiday standard.

Billie Holiday. *Courtesy of the Library of Congress*

## STRANGE FRUIT

By Lewis Allen

*Southern trees bear strange fruit*
*Blood on the leaves and blood at the root*
*Black bodies swinging in the southern breeze*
*Strange fruit hanging from the poplar trees.*

*Pastoral scene of the gallant south*
*The bulging eyes and the twisted mouth*
*Scent of magnolias, sweet and fresh*
*Then the sudden smell of burning flesh.*

*Here is fruit for the crows to pluck*
*For the rain to gather, for the wind to suck*
*For the sun to rot, for the trees to drop*
*Here is a strange and bitter crop.*

The Chicago Children's Choir sings "Strange Fruit," though some people feel it is not suitable for young people. (The song is on the Chicago Children's Choir CD that accompanies this book, *Songs on the Road to Freedom*.) Choir member Anne Wildman admits that the song was hard to sing at first. She feels that it is "important, because it is true and because it is so seldom performed."

Billie Holiday was also apprehensive about performing "Strange Fruit." White America did not want to talk about lynching. It did not want to admit that lynching still occurred. Columbia Records refused to put the song on her album. They thought it was too controversial. Commodore Records agreed to record it. Radio stations refused to play the song.

## Max Roach

Max Roach was one of the all-time great jazz drummers. His career began when he was a boy. His mother was a professional gospel singer. He played the drums in gospel bands from the age of 10.

Roach was born in North Carolina in 1924. His family moved to New York four years later, during the Great Migration. By the time he was 18, Roach was playing with jazz greats. He performed with Dizzy Gillespie, Charlie Parker, Thelonious Monk, Coleman Hawkins, Bud Powell, Charles Mingus, and Miles Davis.

Max Roach rose to become perhaps the greatest drummer of the 20th century. His work was creative and innovative. He continued to explore different musical paths throughout his life. In the later years of the century, he worked with rap musicians.

Throughout the 1940s and 1950s, Max Roach recorded many successful albums. In the 1960s, he began to take on political issues in his music. In 1960, he joined forces with Oscar Brown Jr. Together they wrote, composed, and recorded *We Insist! Max Roach's Freedom Now Suite*. Jazz critic Nat Hentoff helped produce the album, and he wrote about it after Roach died in 2007:

> From slavery (the bitterly sardonic "Driva Man") to "Freedom Day" and "Tears for Johannesburg," to the beatings of black students going on at Southern lunch counters, the *Freedom Now Suite* created such a surge of rebellion that it was soon banned in South Africa, to the pleasure of everyone who had been in the studio that day.

The *Freedom Now Suite* was so political and defiant that it got Roach *blacklisted*. A blacklist is a list of people in a particular field or industry who are considered undesirable for some reason, usually political. Many employers, publishers, and producers in that field check the blacklist.

If a person's name is on the list, they will refuse to employ him or her. In the mostly white music industry, this meant that many companies would not produce Max Roach's albums.

## Abbey Lincoln

Abbey Lincoln was born in Chicago in 1930 and raised in Michigan. She graduated from church choirs to jazz and glamour. Her work included modeling, movies, and night-clubs.

Eventually, she rejected the glamour-girl roles that the entertainment industry offered. "They put me in a Marilyn Monroe–type dress," she said years later, "and I sang the more titillating standards and phony folk tunes, and they told me 'not o sound like a Negro.'" Lincoln began wearing her hair in a *natural* in the 1950s. A natural is a black hairstyle that does not use chemical hair treatments. Abbey Lincoln was ahead of her time. Until the late 1960s, straightened or "processed" hair was considered more beautiful by white culture and by most black people as well.

During the 1960s, she and Max Roach were partners in marriage and music. Abbey Lincoln performed on Roach's *Freedom Now Suite*. Years later, she recalled the civil rights movement: "Nina Simone was singing, 'To Be Young, Gifted and Black.' It was a time when Dr. King was on the stump. We did some things for Malcolm X and

for Dr. King, even though I never met Dr. King. It was a movement that helped all our lives."

## Louis Armstrong

Louis Armstrong played the cornet. Then he moved on to the trumpet. Finally, he became a vocalist. All along the way, Louis Armstrong was a leading jazz musician. Born into poverty in New Orleans in 1901, he grew up in and out of reform school. He started performing in the band of the New Orleans Home for Colored Waifs. *Waifs* are homeless children who have been either abandoned or

Louis Armstrong. *Courtesy of the Library of Congress*

orphaned. In the 1920s, Armstrong headed for Chicago, where the jazz scene was hot. His music took him around the country and the world.

Some black people criticized Louis Armstrong because he performed for segregated audiences. He did not often speak out about civil rights, but he donated money to support the movement. "I don't get involved in politics," he once said. "I just blow my horn."

Then, in 1957, he spoke out—loud and clear. In Little Rock, black students were attacked when they tried to attend the white high school. Armstrong called President Eisenhower "gutless" because he did not act quickly to send troops to defend the teenage students.

At that time, Armstrong was scheduled to tour Russia. The U.S. government sponsored his tour. The government wanted to show a good side of America to the Russian people. Armstrong canceled the tour.

"The people over there ask me what's wrong with my country. What am I supposed to say?" he asked a reporter. "The way they're treating my people in the South, the government can go to hell."

# Folk Songs of Protest

*Folk songs* are based on traditional music. They are the music of the common people. People sing folk songs, including love songs and work songs. (Religious songs—particularly church songs—are not usually considered folk music.) Folk songs are passed down from person to person. Folk music flows from many communities and countries.

For many years, folk music was not popular in the United States. The people most interested in folk songs were historians and professors.

A folk music revival began in the 1950s. Musicians playing folk music became more popular. They composed new songs in the style of traditional folk tunes. Some said the new songs were not really folk music. Others agreed with jazz musician Louis Armstrong. "All music is folk music," he said. "I ain't never heard a horse sing a song."

Folk musicians marched and sang for the civil rights movement. They sang old songs of protest. They invented new ones.

## Lead Belly

Huddy "Lead Belly" Ledbetter was a black folk musician who died in 1949. He sang gospel and blues as well as folk songs. He wrote songs, too. He wrote some songs about racism and political issues. One of his songs protested the unfair convictions of the Scottsboro Boys in 1931.

Lead Belly was invited to Washington to record songs for the Library of Congress. After the recording session, a group went out to dinner to celebrate. They were an interracial group. The restaurant refused to serve them. Afterward, Lead Belly wrote the "Bourgeois Blues." The song bitterly commented on racism in Washington:

Huddy "Lead Belly" Ledbetter and Martha Promise Ledbetter. *Courtesy of the Library of Congress*

"Some white folk in Washington, they know just how, / Call a colored man a nigger just to see him bow. / Lord, it's a bourgeois town." *Bourgeois* means middle-class and respectable. Many people, including Lead Belly, used the word to refer to people who care more about money and respectability than about humanity.

## Woody Guthrie

Woody Guthrie and Pete Seeger were among the singers who learned from Lead Belly. Woody Guthrie's singing life lasted from the Great Depression of the 1930s through the anticommunist era of the 1950s. During the 1960s, he was disabled by Huntington's disease, which ended his life in 1967.

Traveling through the Dust Bowl—a huge region of the United States that suffered from severe drought and widespread poverty in the 1930s—Woody Guthrie sang songs of working people. From Oklahoma to Texas to California, he wrote and sang protest songs. He sang for working people of all races. His songs expressed his belief in civil rights for all people.

In 1940, Woody Guthrie wrote his most famous song, "This Land Is Your Land." His original lyrics express political messages. These lyrics are left out by many singers. Most people have never heard verses 3 and 5.

### THIS LAND IS YOUR LAND

By Woody Guthrie

Chorus:
*This land is your land, this land is my land*
*From California to the New York Island*
*From the Redwood Forest, to the Gulf Stream waters*
*This land was made for you and me*

*As I went walking that ribbon of highway*
*And saw above me that endless skyway*
*And saw below me the golden valley, I said*
*This land was made for you and me*

Woody Guthrie. *Al Aumuller, courtesy of the Library of Congress*

Chorus

*I roamed and rambled and followed my footsteps*
*To the sparkling sands of her diamond deserts*
*And all around me, a voice was sounding*
*This land was made for you and me*

Chorus

*Was a high wall there that tried to stop me*
*A sign was painted said: Private Property*
*But on the back side it didn't say nothing*
*This land was made for you and me*

Chorus

*When the sun come shining, then I was strolling*
*In wheat fields waving and dust clouds rolling*
*The voice was chanting as the fog was lifting*
*This land was made for you and me*

Chorus

*One bright sunny morning in the shadow of the steeple*
*By the Relief Office I saw my people*
*As they stood hungry, I stood there wondering if*
*This land was made for you and me*

Chorus

*Copyrights* protect written work and songs. They prevent people from using someone else's work without paying for it. Woody Guthrie wrote:

> This song is Copyrighted in U.S., under Seal of Copyright #154085, for a period of 28 years, and anybody caught singin' it without our permission, will be mighty good friends of ourn, cause we don't give a dern. Publish it. Write it. Sing it. Swing to it. Yodel it. We wrote it, that's all we wanted to do.

Another of Woody Guthrie's songs mourned the deaths of 28 undocumented farm workers in 1948. They were being deported when their plane crashed. Newspaper stories gave the names of the pilot and crew of the plane. The Mexican workers were just called "deportees." They were buried, nameless, in a mass grave. Woody Guthrie invented names for them: "Goodbye to my Juan, goodbye Rosalita; / Adiós, mis amigos, Jesús y María. . . . / Who are all these friends, all scattered like dry leaves? / The radio says, 'They are just deportees.'"

## Odetta

Odetta grew up in California, and started her musical career as a teenager. From the age of 13, she sang in musicals. In 1950, at the age of 20, she changed direction. The young black woman from Birmingham and Los Angeles fell in love with folk music. Her career gained power with folk and blues recordings, some with jazz styling. Like so many other folk singers, she traveled to sing at rallies and marches and protests. She sang "I'm On My Way" at the March on Washington in 1963.

## Joan Baez

Joan Baez traveled to the South and sang in churches and at rallies in the early 1960s. She sang "Oh, Freedom" at the 1963 March on Washington. At that time, she was 22 years old.

Joan Baez brought her voice and guitar to the movement very early. In 1956, the 15-year-old Baez first heard Martin Luther King Jr. speak. In the same year, she bought her first guitar. Her passion for music was never separate from her passion for justice.

Like many singers, Joan Baez is hard to classify. She is a folk musician, but she also sings popular songs and world music. She recorded an album entirely in Spanish. This album included "*No nos moveran*," the Spanish version of "We Shall Not Be Moved." Best known in this country as a civil rights song, "We Shall Not Be Moved" became popular during the 1950s and 1960s. Yet it is also a protest song in Spain. During the years of dictatorship in Spain, Generalissimo Francisco Franco banned this song.

Besides singing in the civil rights movement, Joan Baez sang in the antiwar movement in the Vietnam War era. She also sang against the torture and murder of the Pinochet dictatorship in Chile.

## Peter, Paul and Mary

In the early 1960s, Peter Yarrow had graduated from Cornell with a degree in psychology. Paul Stookey had graduated from the University of Michigan and was working as a stand-up comic. They met in New York's Greenwich Village. After growing up in Greenwich Village and singing with Pete Seeger, Mary Travers joined Peter and Paul in 1961. They became the folk group Peter, Paul and Mary, and they stayed together for over 45 years.

"We've always been involved with issues that deal with the fundamental human rights of people, whether that means the right to political freedom or the right to breathe air that's clean," says Mary Travers. "If I Had a Hammer," on their first album, is one of their protest songs:

*I've got a hammer, and I've got a bell*
*And I've got a song to sing all over this land*
*It's the hammer of justice, it's the bell of freedom*
*It's a song about love between my brothers and my sisters all*
*over this land.*

Peter, Paul and Mary sang "Blowin' in the Wind" by Bob Dylan (see "Rock and Pop Music," below) at the March on Washington.

## Phil Ochs

Born in 1940, Phil Ochs was a folk singer, but he is better known as a writer of protest songs. He once said that his songs came from *Newsweek*—they were focused on the events of his time. Phil Ochs suffered from alcoholism and manic depression. He killed himself in 1976.

Right after the assassination of Medgar Evers in 1963 (see chapter 5), Ochs wrote a song in his memory. The song said that the bullet "struck the heart of every man when Evers fell and died." That song eventually became "Too Many Martyrs":

*Too many martyrs and too many dead*
*Too many lies too many empty words were said*
*Too many times for too many angry men*
*Oh, let it never be again.*

Ochs also wrote about segregation, "From Birmingham to Harlem's ground, / From Jackson to Chicago's shores," in "Colored Town":

*Just across the railroad tracks*
*On the far side of the town*
*All the people there are black*
*And they live in colored town*

## Rhythm and Blues and Soul Music

People have different definitions of *rhythm and blues* (R&B) and *soul music*. Maybe R&B started in the 1940s. Or maybe it was just a new name for what used to be called *race music*, meaning music recorded by black artists for sale to black people. Did R&B die in the 1960s? Was soul music its successor or just another name for pop music? Or are the names meaningless except for marketing? Music historians do not agree.

Both R&B and soul music are rooted in black musical traditions. Black musicians are their greatest artists. Many gave time, talent, and money to the civil rights movement. They marched and spoke out and sang their songs. In the late 1960s, the songs became more political.

## Sam Cooke

Sam Cooke was born in Mississippi in 1931, the son of a Baptist minister. The family moved to Chicago in 1933, and Cooke grew up there, singing in the church and in gospel groups. In 1956, he began to sing R&B songs, recording 29 Top 40 hits before his death in 1964.

Sam Cooke wrote "A Change Is Gonna Come" for the civil rights movement.

*I go to the movie, and I go downtown*
*Somebody keep telling me "Don't hang around"*
*It's been a long time coming*
*But I know a change is gonna come.*

## Curtis Mayfield

Born in Chicago in 1942, Curtis Mayfield wrote songs and sang with the Impressions singing group during the 1960s. "Keep On Pushin'," "People Get Ready," "Choice of Colors," "This Is My Country," and "Check Out Your Mind" expressed the feelings and desires of the times.

The Rock and Roll Hall of Fame honored Curtis Mayfield twice. He was recognized as a member of the Impressions. He also won honors for his solo career. The Hall of Fame praised him for "couching social commentary and keenly observed black-culture archetypes in funky, danceable rhythms." His songs became more political during the late 1960s and beyond. Starting with civil rights, his compositions grew to take on a range of social issues.

Mayfield's songs denounced "educated fools from uneducated schools" and warned that "if there's a hell below, we're all gonna go." He also held out hope, insisting that "we're a winner" and "we're movin' on up."

In one interview, Mayfield explained how politics and song came together. "It wasn't hard to take notice of segregation and the struggle for equality at this time," he said.

These were the issues that concerned me as a young black man. So it was easy to write songs that might prove to be inspiring or give food for thought like "Keep on Pushing," "Choice of Colors" or take on the gospel hymns like "Amen." In fact, "Keep on Pushing" was a perfect example of what has laid in my subconscious for years—the musical strands and themes of gospel singers and preachers that I'd heard as a child.

## Mavis Staples

Mavis Staples began singing with her family gospel group at the age of 11. She graduated from high school in 1957. Then the Staples Singers—Mavis, Cleo, Yvonne, Pervis, and their father—took the show on the road. As the civil rights movement grew, they moved with it. Mavis remembers her father saying that if Dr. King could preach it, they could sing it. They sang "message" songs, such as "Long Walk to D.C." Their songs repeatedly hit the Top 40.

Mavis Staples went on to a successful solo career. She never left her gospel roots. She never left her political commitments either. In 2007, she recorded *We'll Never Turn Back*, a CD of songs from the civil rights movement and today. As record producer Andy Kaulkin said, "The Staples Singers were doing freedom songs before there was a term [for] 'freedom songs.'"

A long list of R&B and soul musicians supported the civil rights movement.

At the same time, the black pride and black power movement grew. Aretha Franklin recorded "Respect." James Brown sang "Say It Loud—I'm Black and I'm Proud." For six weeks, it stayed at the top of the rhythm and blues singles chart, and made it to number 10 on the Billboard Hot 100.

## Nina Simone

Nina Simone (1933–2003) never wanted to be classified. Most people called her a jazz musician. Some called her a soul singer. She preferred the term *black classical music*. She said that jazz was the classical music of black people. She was a pianist, singer, and songwriter.

When Nina Simone was 10 years old, she performed a classical piano recital. Her parents came and sat in the front row. They were forced to move to the back to make room for white people. She refused to play until they were seated in front again.

Nina Simone was active in the civil rights movement. She spoke and sang at civil rights marches. She recorded songs such as "Mississippi Goddam," which she released in 1964 as a protest against the assassination of Medgar Evers. In "Old Jim Crow," she sang about how ending legal segregation was just a first step toward ending the Jim Crow system of segregation.

*Old Jim Crow*
*I thought I had you beat*
*Now I see you walkin'*
*And talkin' up and down my street*

## Stax Records

Stax Records was founded in 1957 by a white brother and sister, Jim Stewart and Estelle Axton. They started the record company in a garage in Memphis. Soon they moved it to an old movie theater at College and McLemore Avenues. Stax grew to become one of the leading soul music studios. Musicians called the neighborhood around Stax "Soulsville."

Black and white musicians worked together during the early years. Stax musicians included Sam & Dave, Otis Redding, Isaac Hayes, Carla Thomas, Albert King, Wilson Pickett, and Mavis Staples and the Staples Singers. Booker T and the MGs were the house band, and they backed up many of the singers.

After the assassination of Dr. Martin Luther King Jr. in Memphis in 1968, the good feelings between the musicians began to change. Nothing was ever the same again. By 1975, bankruptcy had closed Stax. The record studio was eventually demolished.

Today, in the two Soulsville ZIP codes, 38106 and 38126, nearly 80 percent of the children live in single-parent homes. Poverty rates are among the country's highest.

In the early 21st century, private donors and public agencies joined to bring Stax back. Together, they turned the vacant patch of land at McLemore and College into a multimillion-dollar, state-of-the-art Stax Museum of American Soul Music.

Next to the museum, the Stax Music Academy was created. More than 350 young people go there each year for after-school and summer programs. The Soulsville Charter School, located in the same building, offers academic challenge to neighborhood children.

# Rock and Pop Music

Rock and pop musicians also gave voice to the struggle for justice and freedom. Sometimes the lines between folk

Chicago Children's Choir in front of Stax Records in Memphis, Tennessee. *Davin Peelle*

and pop music blurred, but many musicians made clear their commitment to the civil rights movement and to the peace movement.

## Bob Dylan

Bob Dylan grew up in northern Minnesota. He joined bands while he was in high school. One was called the Shadow Blasters, and another was the Golden Chords. The Golden Chords performed at a high school talent show. They were so loud that the principal cut off the microphone.

Attending the University of Minnesota, Dylan sang in bars and coffeehouses. By 1961, he had moved to New York. He spent time there learning from folk singer Woody Guthrie. Dylan became one of the best-known protest singers of the 1960s.

Dylan's "Blowin' in the Wind" from 1963 brought together issues of racism and peace, asking: "How many roads must a man walk down, / Before you call him a man?" and "How many times must the cannon balls fly, / Before they're forever banned?"

A year later, "The Times They Are A-Changin'" struck a chord with protesters everywhere. In the song, Dylan called on mothers and fathers to listen to their children, who are now "beyond your command." He warned that there was a "battle outside, and it's raging." He told writers to keep their eyes open, because "the chance won't come again."

Some of Dylan's songs focused specifically on civil rights issues. "Oxford Town" was about James Meredith's entry into the University of Mississippi. Meredith broke the segregation there as the first black student ever at "Ole Miss." Dylan also wrote "The Death of Emmett Till," in memory of the 14-year-old murdered in Mississippi in 1955. He took a turn on stage at the March on Washington.

## Janis Ian

Janis Ian was born in 1951, and was only 12 years old when she wrote her first song. That song was released in 1965 on the same album with her biggest hit: "Society's Child." "Society's Child" stirred instant controversy. Some disc jockeys were fired for playing it. One radio station was burned down.

What kind of song could stir such passion? "Society's Child" was a story of interracial teenage romance. The song told the story of the reactions of parents, teachers, and classmates to a teenage romance between a young white woman and a young black man. It is sung in the voice of the young woman. In the song, she ends the relationship. She is, after all, just "society's child," and cannot resist society's pressure.

In 1965, laws still prohibited interracial marriage throughout the South. Any hint of interest in a white woman by a black man or boy in the South made him an instant target. Beating, tarring and feathering, and death were the penalties imposed by lynch mobs.

Northern states generally did not have laws against interracial marriage. This does not mean that interracial romance was easy. As in the song, most of society strongly disapproved. Interracial couples, young or old, faced extreme prejudice.

Like most pop and rock singers, Janis was young during the civil rights movement. Her songs reflected her passionate commitment to equality and justice. "Younger Generation Blues," released on the same album, spoke for many.

## Handling Racism with a Kiss

The Chicago Children's Choir began touring in 1965. Their first trip took them to Des Moines, Tulsa, and St. Louis. In Tulsa, the racially integrated choir purposefully went into the African American community to sing at all-black schools. Choir director Chris Moore said that this symbolic act had a profound "impact on the Tulsa community." From Tulsa to St. Louis, the children confronted the harsh reality of accommodations that "were not prepared to deal with integrated groups."

During one tour, children visited Mammoth Cave in Kentucky. While they were exploring the cave, a tourist, offended by the racial integration of the choir, snapped at a 13-year-old singer, "Nigger Lover!" The girl was upset and angry. According to Moore, she "wanted to do something, and she waited for her moment . . . until the whole group on that walking tour gathered around in a large, better lit . . . place. She then picked one of the really handsome young black men in our group, and went over to wind herself around him and gave him one hell of a kiss." Chris Moore characterized this courageous and defiant act as "standing for the integrity of what we were about, and handling racism in a unique way."

*If you think I'm hating grown-ups*
*You've got me all wrong*
*They're very nice people*
*When they stay where they belong.*

She believed that her generation could change the world. With controversy came success. She traveled across the country in concert tours. Ella Fitzgerald called her "the best young singer in America." After three intense years in the spotlight, Ian "retired" at age 18. She came back three years later, and is still going strong.

Like Janis Ian, other young people made music a huge part of their lives. They also worked for civil rights, for peace, and for justice for all people. From jazz to soul to rock 'n' roll, secular music contributed to the civil rights movement.

Chapter 7

South Africa

*Kwangena thina bo,*

*We Mame!*

*Kwashay' umoya*

*When we enter,*

*Oh, Mama!*

*The spirit is moved*

*Lizela, a traditional Xhosa song*

The U.S. civil rights movement shared much with South Africa's antiapartheid movement. Both movements struggled to end discrimination and segregation. Both shared common dreams of justice and equality. People in South Africa were inspired by the struggle in the United States, and people in the U.S. civil rights movement spoke out against apartheid in South Africa. Each movement drew strength from the other.

South Africa was segregated from the time of European conquest in the 1600s. Europeans brought slaves from Asia and from other African countries into South Africa. Over the years, Dutch and English immigrants came to South Africa.

Many different African ethnic groups lived in South Africa before and after the European invasion. The black South Africans never stopped fighting for their rights.

One tribe, the Zulu people, fought and lost the Zulu Wars in the 19th century.

The Dutch settlers spoke a language called *Afrikaans* and called themselves *Afrikaners*. They fought the British for control of South Africa, losing in 1902. In 1910, the British established the Union of South Africa as an independent, white-ruled country.

The native black people of South Africa continued to resist the white European settlers, both British and Dutch. In 1912, they founded the African National Congress (ANC). The goal of the ANC was to end white rule and create a multiracial country. In 1944, Nelson Mandela, Walter Sisulu, and Oliver Tambo formed the ANC Youth League. The Youth League was a more activist organization.

In 1948, the Afrikaner-led National Party came to power. The new government set up a legal system called *apartheid*—an Afrikaans word meaning "apartness." The apartheid system consisted of numerous laws designed to separate people of different races.

Apartheid laws classified people by color. White people had full rights. Black South Africans were called Bantus. Their rights were severely limited. In between, two more groups were identified. "Coloured" people had mixed ancestry. Many were descendants of Asian slaves and black South Africans. Indians (from India) were another class. "Coloured" and Indian people had more rights than black South Africans, but fewer than whites.

Every single person was classified by race. Everyone had to carry an identity document called a *passbook* at all times. The passbook stated the person's race, and race determined where people could live, what jobs they could hold, what schools they could attend, and even whom they could marry.

The apartheid laws said that black South Africans were not even citizens of South Africa. Instead, they were citizens of rural areas called *homelands*. Homelands were barren plots of land where the government had assigned them to live. Many black South Africans had never been to one of these homelands, but under apartheid, that did not matter. Even if they had been born in a city and lived

A South African policeman with a long club chases a black resident during unrest in Langa, near Cape Town, during the successful anti-passbook campaign of March 1960. *Associated Press*

there most of their lives, they had no right to be there and were only allowed to remain on a "temporary" basis.

In 1949, the ANC Youth League called for mass marches, strikes, and protests against apartheid. In 1952, the ANC led a coalition of Indian, coloured, and white organizations in a Campaign of Defiance Against Unjust Laws. The Pan-African Congress (PAC) and the South African Communist Party also worked to end apartheid.

Nelson Mandela was arrested and banned from all political activity under the "Suppression of Communism" law. Later, he and other ANC leaders were charged with treason. Their trials dragged on for years. They were finally found not guilty in 1961.

During the 1950s, black South Africans were "cleared" from some city areas through forced removals. They might have lived in the neighborhood for decades. The law said that did not matter. They could be forcibly removed to a homeland. Tens of thousands of black South Africans lost their homes.

Major movements against apartheid took place in the 1950s, 1960s, 1970s, and 1980s. Each time, the government repressed protest with extreme brutality.

On March 21, 1960, police opened fire on antiapartheid protesters in the black township of Sharpeville. Sixty-nine people were killed—most were shot in the back. The government declared a state of emergency and banned the ANC and other antiapartheid groups.

On March 28, 1960, black South Africans burn their passbooks, a symbol of apartheid control. This protest took place during a "day of mourning" a week after the Sharpeville Massacre. *Associated Press*

Nelson Mandela, African National Congress leader, and Coretta Scott King, widow of slain civil rights leader Martin Luther King Jr., sing and dance at a victory celebration in Johannesburg, May 2, 1994, after Mandela and the ANC took the majority of the votes in the country's first integrated elections. *David Brauchli, Associated Press*

Nelson Mandela was arrested again in 1962. This time he was kept in jail for 30 years.

In 1976, black students in Soweto protested the government's declaration that all students must learn in the Afrikaans language. Soweto, located on the outskirts of the city of Johannesburg, was a segregated, crowded, run-down slum. The government suppressed the Soweto Uprising, killing 575 protesters, including a number of school children, in eight months.

In the 1980s, the antiapartheid struggle turned more violent, with armed uprisings in some townships and bru-

tal police repression. Black South African bishop Desmond Tutu, a leader in the antiapartheid movement, won the Nobel Peace Prize in 1984.

Finally, in 1990, the South African government lifted its ban on the ANC, releasing Mandela and other jailed leaders. The government began negotiations for a multiracial democracy.

Nelson Mandela and South African president F. W. de Klerk represented the two sides in negotiations. They won the Nobel Peace Prize together in 1993. The next year, apartheid officially ended. Nelson Mandela was elected president in free national elections. The ANC won 252 of the 400 seats in parliament.

## Music in South Africa

In South Africa, music played a huge part in organizing the movement against apartheid. Traditional songs were often changed to fit the times, just as happened in the civil rights movement in the United States.

South African music combines two distinct musical cultures. South African traditional music is one part of the mix. This music has extremely complex rhythms. Call-and-response structure may feature one voice and a chorus, or two different groups.

Dance movements are also an important part of South African music. Chupe, a South African musician, explains: "There are certain songs that require some movement and you have to move, and that's a very important part, I think, of any traditional African singing—there has to be movement." His fellow musician Patiswa adds: "If you were to sing the songs without movement . . . the whole song flops. . . . If you have an accompanied piece [of European music], the accompaniment is so *major*. Like if you sing it a cappella, it's not right. So the song without the movement, it just doesn't make sense—*to us*."

The second influence on South African music is the hymns and religious music brought over by missionaries from Europe. These include traditional Christian images. Song text may come from the Bible.

Combining both traditions, South Africa produces powerful choral music. A song may have a European structure with African harmonies woven in. Words may echo the Bible but change with the culture. One example is "*Njengebhadi libhadula.*" The words to this song sound very much like Psalm 42. The psalm says: "As the deer longs for streams of water, so my soul longs for you, O God." The South African song does not mention God directly, but says, "As the antelope longs for the streams of water, so my soul also longs." Although the text comes from a European source, the song uses African rhythms, harmonies, and dance movements.

## Singing to Educate

"Follow the Drinking Gourd" was a song used by slaves in the United States to pass on important information. The "drinking gourd" was a constellation of stars. Also known as the Big Dipper, the constellation included the North Star. Slaves running away to freedom headed north. They followed the drinking gourd and the North Star.

## FOLLOW THE DRINKING GOURD

(Traditional)

*When the sun comes back*
*And the first quail calls*
*Follow the drinking gourd*
*For the old man is waiting*
*For to carry you to freedom*
*If you follow the drinking gourd.*

Chorus:
*Follow the drinking gourd*
*Follow the drinking gourd*
*For the old man is waiting*
*For to carry you to freedom*
*If you follow the drinking gourd.*

*The riverbank will make a very good road*
*The dead trees show you the way*
*Left foot, peg foot traveling on*
*Following the drinking gourd.*

Chorus

*The river ends between two hills*
*Follow the drinking gourd*
*There's another river on the other side*
*Follow the drinking gourd.*

Chorus

*When the great big river meets the little river*
*Follow the drinking gourd*
*For the old man is waiting*
*For to carry you to freedom*
*If you follow the drinking gourd.*

Chorus

Each verse in the song gives specific directions from Alabama to the North. For example, "the old man is waiting" and "peg foot traveling on" refers to Peg Leg Joe, a man who helped slaves to escape on the Underground Railroad, a secret path to freedom for runaway slaves. The river that ends "between two hills" is the Tombigbee River, one of the routes for escape.

During the years of apartheid, South Africans also used songs to educate. They sang about what certain politicians had done. Songs told about unjust laws. They told the stories of suffering of political prisoners.

Today, South Africans face a huge struggle against HIV/AIDS. Acquired Immune Deficiency Syndrome (AIDS) is a disease caused by the Human Immunodeficiency Virus (HIV). The virus attacks the body's immune system, weakening its defenses. HIV is spread through body fluids, especially through sexual activity and through the sharing of contaminated needles by drug users. There is no known cure for AIDS, though some medicines help to fight off its effects.

In South Africa today, about 12 percent of the population is living with HIV. More than 1.5 million children are orphans because of AIDS. Some 400,000 people die from AIDS every year.

Music plays a crucial part in today's struggle against HIV/AIDS. An antiapartheid chant called for taking an AK-47 rifle to fight apartheid. The same chant today calls for using a condom to fight HIV. Another song tells about the ABCs of living with HIV/AIDS. The ABCs are: Abstain, Be faithful, Condomize. Through the song, people are educated about three ways to stop the spread of HIV/AIDS. Another song recalls, "Formerly we needed AK-47s to fight the oppressors. Now—we need knowledge to fight the evil one—HIV."

Old Mutual/Telkom is the largest financial services company in South Africa. Every year, it sponsors a music festival. Singers from all over the country compete.

Tshepo, a South African musician, described the festival:

Mollie Spector Stone, associate conductor of the Chicago Children's Choir and choir alum, has studied extensively in South Africa. She has produced a DVD and book that demonstrate how to teach South African music. *Mary C. Turck*

It's all kind of about what is happening now, it's about reconciliation, it's about people coming together, it's about happiness, it's about love, you know. . . . It's about: people need to be optimistic about what is happening, look into the future. Last year we had the Old Mutual National Choir Festival, and the theme . . . was about love and HIV and AIDS, to actually educate people about love, to educate people to have one partner, and to educate people about the dangers about HIV and AIDS. And then, most of the choirs had to prepare a song . . . which was composed for the competition, which I think was a great thing, because, you see, in each province . . . you get about 10,000 of people coming for one competition—so actually *by music*, you're able to spread about the dangers of HIV to people." (Interview with Tshepo, in *Vela, Vela*, copyright 2004 by Mollie Spector Stone. Used with permission.)

## Singing to Protest

Songs of protest were a huge part of the civil rights movement in the United States. They were also sung during apartheid in South Africa. People sang songs to protest the government's policies and laws. The famous song *"Senzeni na?"* asks "What have we done to deserve this treatment, except be black?"

People in South Africa today sing this same song back at the government. Today they are singing about the struggle against HIV. They ask, "What have we done to deserve this treatment, except be black? What have we done to deserve this treatment, except have HIV?"

People also sing songs protesting the high price of medicines. Songs ask the drug companies to provide generic versions of the medicines needed to fight HIV. People sing songs asking the government to provide medicine to pregnant women and to prisoners. They sing songs about false information about HIV/AIDS coming from the health minister.

Ncumisa, a South African musician, explained:

> We can never stop singing the political songs, because even though the songs were about the struggle then, there are other struggles now—economic, social . . . so people will always be singing those songs. We are younger now; we didn't really experience the struggle [against apartheid] that much. So yes, we sing the songs; yes, we recognize that these are songs that kept people going. But it's like we've injected something *else* in it—a sort of "joy." (Interview with Ncumisa, in *Vela, Vela*, copyright 2004 by Mollie Spector Stone. Used with permission.)

## Singing to Comfort People

Singing uplifts the spirits of people who are suffering. Slaves in the United States sang about better days to come. Civil rights protesters, facing dogs and clubs and water hoses, sang to keep up their courage. In jail, they sang to comfort each other.

Vuyisile Mini was born in South Africa in 1920. He organized workers into unions. He fought against removal of black people from the cities. He was a leader in the trade union movement and in the ANC. He was also a composer, a poet, and a singer.

Some of his songs expressed protest:

*Verwoerd pasopa*
*Naants' indod' emnyama*

*Look out, Verwoerd*
*Here are the black people*

Verwoerd was the white leader of South Africa who enforced apartheid.

In 1956, Mini was jailed and charged with treason. He wrote another song to comfort the people in prison with him:

*Thath' umthwalo Buti sigoduke*
*Balindile oomama noo bab' ekhaya*

*Take up your things, brother, and let's go*
*They are waiting, our mothers and fathers, at home*

After years in prison, Mini was acquitted and released, but in 1963 he was jailed again. He and two fellow activists were sentenced to death. Another ANC leader was in prison with them when Mini and his two coworkers were executed. He wrote about their last moments:

> The last evening was devastatingly sad as the heroic occupants of the death cells communicated to the prison population in gentle melancholy song that their end was near. . . . It was late at night when the singing ceased, and the prison fell into uneasy silence.
>
> I was already awake when the singing began again in the early morning. Once again the excruciatingly beautiful music floated through the barred windows, echoing round the brick exercise yard, losing itself in the vast prison yards.
>
> And then, unexpectedly, the voice of Vuyisile Mini came roaring down the hushed passages. Evidently standing on a stool, with his face reaching up to a barred vent in his cell, his unmistakable bass voice was enunciating his final message in Xhosa [an African language] to the world he was leaving. In a voice charged with emotion but stubbornly defiant he spoke of the struggle waged by the African National Congress and of his absolute conviction of the victory to come. And then it was Khayinga's turn, followed by Mkaba, as they too defied all prison rules to shout out their valedictions.
>
> Soon after, I heard the door of their cell being opened. Murmuring voices reached my straining ears, and then the three martyrs broke into a final poignant melody which seemed to fill the whole prison with sound and

then gradually faded away into the distant depths of the condemned section.

Singing continues to comfort people in South Africa today. One powerful example is the choir called Siphitemba. The name Siphitemba means "we give hope." The choir members are all *HIV positive*—they have been diagnosed with the virus.

Being HIV positive carries a terrible stigma in South Africa. People are afraid to tell their families. They fear being disowned or shunned. They also feel that being HIV positive is a death sentence.

Siphitemba helps people who are HIV positive. When someone is diagnosed, the choir sings to him or her. The song says, "You are not dying of HIV, you are living with HIV." Another song offers religious comfort. This song promises, "Jesus was here yesterday, he is here today and he will get us through the struggle, and he will be here tomorrow."

Choir members accompany the person who is now living with HIV. They sing songs of hope and comfort to the family. And they welcome the person into the choir. Anyone who is HIV positive can be a member of the choir.

## Singing to Preserve Cultural Identity

Hollywood is everywhere in the world, selling movies and music and television shows and personalities across the globe. International corporations sell the same hamburgers, the same shoes, the same shirts around the world. Many believe that this global culture is now, and traditional cultures are yesterday or last year. Music helps to break through this prejudice. As carriers of culture, musicians move around the world. They sing out the richness of their own cultures.

South African reggae artist Lucky Dube was born in a small town west of Johannesburg. In 1982, at the age of 18, he made his first album, *Lucky Dube and the Supersoul.* Dube combined traditional Zulu rhythms with political messages. In 1985, the South African government banned his *Rasta Never Die* album. After apartheid ended, Dube became an international star. His songs, in Zulu, English, and Afrikaans, reflected the cultures of South Africa.

Lucky Dube was gunned down in Johannesburg in 2007. Messages of mourning came from Panama, the Solomon Islands, Sudan, India, the United States—from around the world. They showed his success in bringing South African culture to the world.

## Singing in Solidarity

In the 1980s, people around the world awakened to the antiapartheid struggle. Students and politicians in many countries tried to pressure the South African government. People organized to educate. They spread the word about the cruelty of apartheid. They declared their solidarity with the antiapartheid movement. Musicians and artists declared a "cultural boycott" of South Africa. They refused to perform in the country or allow their works to be performed there as long as the apartheid system continued.

Musicians stood in the forefront of this solidarity movement. In England, "Free Nelson Mandela" became a Top 10 rock song. In the mid-1980s, musician Paul Simon visited South Africa to record music with South African artists. Some people criticized him for breaking the cultural boycott. Others defended him, noting that he offered no support to the South African government. All of his work was with black South African musicians.

Simon featured the South African singing group Ladysmith Black Mambazo on his *Graceland* album. He also helped them to record the album *Shaka Zulu.* In effect, he introduced the group to global audiences. *Shaka Zulu* won the 1987 Grammy for Best Traditional Folk Recording.

Hugh Masekela is a South African jazz musician. He began playing the trumpet as a teenager. In the 1950s, he played with dance and jazz bands. Then, in 1960, the government killed 69 protesters in the Sharpeville Massacre. Afterward, the government banned gatherings of 10 or more people. With apartheid becoming more restrictive, Masekela left South Africa. He studied music in England, and also visited the United States. His hits during the 1960s included "Grazin' in the Grass" and "Up, Up and Away."

Masekela did not forget his home. In 1987, he recorded "Bring Him Back Home." This song was part of the global antiapartheid movement. The hit single demanded Nelson Mandela's release from prison. Masekela toured with Paul Simon. He began to return to his African musical roots. In the 1980s, he moved to Botswana, just across the South African border. In his studio there, he connected with South African musicians. In the 1990s, he was finally able to return to South Africa.

Miriam Makeba is also known as "Mama Africa." Born in South Africa in 1932, she began singing in the 1950s. Makeba sang both jazz and traditional South African melodies. She starred in *Come Back, Africa* in 1959. This antiapartheid documentary won international fame.

Makeba attended the film's opening in Italy. She decided not to return home. Living outside the country, she sang and spoke about the evils of apartheid. The South African government revoked her passport, banned her music, and finally revoked her citizenship.

In 1990, Nelson Mandela asked her to return to South Africa, and she did.

Sun City was a South African interracial gambling resort. It also became a symbol of musical solidarity. Sun City sat in the middle of a poverty-stricken rural homeland. Many musicians agreed to boycott Sun City. They refused to perform at Sun City in order to protest apartheid.

In 1987, Bruce Springsteen and Miles Davis recorded *Sun City*. This album was a strong antiapartheid protest. Fifty-four other musicians joined in for parts of the album. Both the album and a hit single were called "Sun City."

The song was very political. In part, its lyrics said:

*Relocation to phony homelands*
*Separation of families I can't understand*
*Twenty-three million can't vote because they're black*
*We're stabbing our brothers and sisters in the back.*
Sun City, *Steven Van Zandt (Blue Midnight Music, 1985)*

The song also criticized U.S. president Ronald Reagan. It said he had failed to take strong action against the South African government. Because of this criticism, about half of all U.S. radio stations refused to play *Sun City*.

# After Apartheid: Chicago Children's Choir in South Africa

In 1996, after the end of apartheid, the Chicago Children's Choir visited South Africa. They came for a five-week concert tour. Choir members stayed in people's homes. They met people of widely varied social and economic standing and people of all races. They discovered a country still deeply divided.

"The townships were so separate from everything else," one choir member recalled. "These white people lived in South Africa and didn't know anything about black people's lives except that these were their maids. They had never been into a black township—and we [choir members] had. That was so odd to us."

While the tour was occasionally scary, it was also exhilarating. People were still singing antiapartheid songs, but now with a real sense of success. One South African friend told a choir member, "Now we can sing these songs and enjoy them, because we won!"

Mollie Stone was a junior in high school when she went on the tour. It transformed her life. Mollie became a professional musician. She returned to South Africa to study its music and people. In time, Mollie became the associate conductor of the Chicago Children's Choir.

"In South Africa," Mollie said in 2007, "music is this incredible tool that people use to create change in their world. Through singing, they preserve their cultural iden- tity, resist oppression, and fight for freedom."

Mollie loves and teaches South African music. She says this is different from teaching Western choral music. "South African music is too complex to be notated using Western notation, unless you simplify it," she explains.

People were very happy to simplify songs to make them more accessible. But this pattern is destructive because in simplifying the music, people play into the misconcep- tion that everything African is "primitive and simplistic," when in fact it is *too* complicated for our notation sys-

tem, with its rhythms, different sense of tuning, and dance movements.

So Mollie teaches South African music as it is taught and learned there. "South African music is taught and learned in the oral tradition—that's an act of creating community itself. You are watching each other, listening to each other. You are creating community in singing and learning, not burying your face in a piece of paper."

★   ★   ★   ★   ★

## Mollie Stone Remembers the CCC Tour

"We had prepared all of this music, including South African music. But none of us understood how anyone overthrew the government using music that sounded so simple and uninterest- ing to us.

"The way we learned the songs was very different from how they were sung in South Africa. We learned it all from the written page. When the music was transcribed, they made it really sim- ple. We didn't really understand how it was supposed to sound.

"While on tour, we sang in a black township. At one point, our conductor said to the audience, 'Now we are going to sing a song that is South African.' I felt so humiliated—I didn't want to sing the song for them, because I knew we didn't really *feel* it. We didn't really understand it. Embarrassingly, the video of that concert captures me rolling my eyes.

"Then the students in the audience were invited to sing.

"I remember thinking—these kids can't just burst into four-part harmony. But they did! They just got up and sang with so much spirit. It was so different from what we had learned. Within two minutes they got us all off the stage, took us by the hand, and we were dancing. It felt like it went on for hours. We were so happy. And we finally understood how powerfully the music created a sense of community. Through that song, we felt deeply connected to the people with whom we were singing.

"I felt totally exhilarated by understanding finally: that's how they used this music to overthrow apartheid. It's so beautiful, so powerful, that it's terrifying in a way—to see people so in tune with each other.

"Then I felt totally betrayed. I thought, how can I come from this wealthy, privileged country with so many resources, and not have had any way to learn how this music really sounds? Everything that is powerful and exciting in South African music was sucked out of it when it was written down in America. I devoted the next years of my life to figuring out why that was, and how to fix it."

## Chapter 8

The Movement Continues

*Ain't gonna let nobody turn me around*
*Turn me around, turn me around*
*Ain't gonna let nobody turn me around*
*Gonna keep on a'walkin, keep on a'talkin*
*Gonna build a brand-new world.*

Forty years after the assassination of Dr. Martin Luther King Jr., the civil rights movement continues. Activists still work to build that brand-new world. Like the songs of the 1960s, the words change but the melody remains the same. The melody of the movement is a powerful drumbeat for justice.

During the 1960s, the drum beat for racial equality. That theme still sounds today. Over the past forty years, other voices have joined the chorus. Women, Mexican farm workers, Native Americans, gay men, lesbian women, bisexual and transgendered people, immigrants, old people, young people, people with disabilities—all these voices sound their own calls for equality. Around the world, oppressed people struggle for justice and equality.

In the 1960s, children, teenagers, and young adults put their lives on the line in the civil rights movement. Young people took on their shoulders the burden and responsibility of leadership in the movement. Today, too, young people stand with their elders in movements for justice and equality. Schools are still a place for organizing and action on issues ranging from peace to human rights, from racism to religion.

Chicago Children's Choir singers pledge their commitment to justice at a wall of the Civil Rights Memorial in Montgomery, Alabama. The wall says " . . . until justice rolls down like waters and righteousness like a mighty stream." *Davin Peelle*

# Standing Up for Free Speech in Schools

In 1965, Mary Beth Tinker was one of six children of a Methodist preacher in Des Moines, Iowa. Her father and mother had gone to Mississippi in 1964. They went there to work for civil rights with the Southern Christian Leadership Conference.

In 1965, civil rights and the war in Vietnam came together for many people. That fall, students planned to protest the war. They decided to wear black armbands to school. The armbands symbolized mourning for the dead on both sides of the war. The Des Moines school board threatened to suspend anyone who wore an armband. "I decided to wear the armband anyway," says Tinker. "We each have to make those decisions in life." She and four others were suspended in mid-December.

Some people threatened the Tinker family. Some sent hate mail. A phone caller on Christmas Eve threatened to bomb their house.

The school board said that the students could not come back as long as they wore armbands. By the end of the winter break, the students had a solution. They took off the armbands. Instead, they wore all black clothing for the rest of the school year.

The Des Moines students and their parents sued the school board. They said that wearing armbands was free speech. In 1969, the Supreme Court said the students were right. The First Amendment protected their right to protest. The school was wrong when it ordered them to remove the armbands. Students' rights, the court said, do not stop at the schoolhouse door.

Tinker became a nurse and continued her activism. She speaks to students and tells them: "Kids can shake things up! That's what we need today—to shake things up!" When she speaks in schools, Tinker brings a recording of Nina Simone's "Backlash Blues." The song was written by black poet Langston Hughes. It includes the lines:

*Mr. Backlash, Mr. Backlash*
*Just who do you think I am?*
*You raise my taxes, freeze my wages*
*And send my son to Vietnam.*

For Tinker, the issues of the 21st century seem like the issues that Nina Simone sang about in the 1960s.

## Students Organizing in Schools

In Mississippi in 1958, 15-year-old James Chaney went to a segregated high school. He was a youth member of the NAACP, and he wanted to recruit other youth members. He and two other young people decided to wear paper badges with the letters "NAACP" to school.

Their principal suspended the three young organizers for a week. He said he would suspend any student who wore a badge. He was afraid of the white school board, and probably afraid of any student organizing as well.

Badges, buttons, and black armbands are no longer issues for schools in the 21st century. Today, the battles for students' rights focus on clubs and associations.

Schools try to avoid controversy. They know that no one will object to a chess club. Political organizing is different. Politics and religion are "hot button" issues. People have strong feelings about both. The easy way out is for a school to ban all religious and political groups. But the law says that public high schools cannot take the easy way out.

In 1984, Congress passed the Equal Access Act. This law says that public high schools must treat student groups equally. Schools may not discriminate against student groups because of their political or religious beliefs. The law applies only to secondary schools. It applies to groups that are started, sponsored, and led by students—not by outsiders.

The law only prohibits discrimination. Schools may ban *all* non-curriculum-related groups. They may not ban only those they consider controversial.

A SNCC poster in the 1960s reminded people what was at stake: "One Man, One Vote."
*McCain Library and Archives, University of Southern Mississippi*

119

## Bible Clubs

Religious clubs sometimes face opposition from school authorities. In 1993, Emily Hsu asked permission for the Walking on Water Student Christian Fellowship to meet at her school. The club's constitution said that its officers had to be Christian. The school said this violated nondiscrimination policies.

Emily Hsu sued the school district. In 1996, a federal court decided that the club could meet at the school. In this and other cases, courts say that all student groups must be treated alike. If a school allows a chess club to meet at school, then a religious or political club should also be allowed to meet.

## Gay-Straight Alliances

In the 21st century, many student struggles focus on gender and identity. Lesbian, gay, bisexual, and transgendered (LGBT) students report harassment and bullying. A 2005 study showed that three out of four LGBT students often heard biased remarks and name-calling. More than one-third had experienced physical harassment because of their sexual orientation.

*We are a gentle angry people*
*Singing, singing for our lives*

by Holly Near, Copyright 1979 Hereford Music

## Chicago, 2006

Jorge Mena and Heather Hall were seniors at the Noble Street Charter High School in Chicago. They founded a gay-straight alliance to promote "awareness, safety, respect and tolerance of all sexual orientations." The school said they could not be an official group. They sued to get equal standing. In 2006, the school agreed to settle the case.

The GSA now must be treated the same as any other group. They may have access to meeting space. They may advertise their meetings on campus. And they may be included in the school yearbook.

Holly Near's "Singing for Our Lives" comes from the movement for equality for lesbian, gay, bisexual, and transgendered people. Holly Near wrote it after the assassination of a gay politician. Supervisor Harvey Milk and Mayor George Moscone were assassinated in San Francisco in 1978. Harvey Milk was gay. He and Moscone were killed by an antigay former city official.

Gay-straight alliance (GSA) groups try to combat bigotry based on sexual orientation and gender identity in their schools. Schools find GSA groups even scarier than Bible clubs. From Lubbock, Texas, to Chicago, Illinois, schools have banned GSA groups. Courts have ruled repeatedly that GSA groups are protected by law.

## Youth Against War and Racism

In 2004, three high school students decided to organize against military recruiting in their school. The students distributed antirecruiting literature in the lunchroom. They also set up a display table in the lunchroom at the same time that the military recruiters were there.

The American Legion complained to the principal and school district. The school ordered the students to take down their table. The students insisted that they had a right to a table. Eventually, the school agreed that they had a legal right to be there.

The long tradition of student organizing continues across the country. Politics and religion, war and racism, LGBT rights, and environmental issues are among top student concerns at the beginning of the 21st century.

## Black America in the 21st Century

In Mississippi in 1960, people lived in black or white neighborhoods. Students went to black or white schools.

Jobs, seats on the bus, water fountains, lunch counters—all were assigned by race. White schools were better schools. White jobs paid higher wages. White neighborhoods had better housing. The law established and enforced segregation.

Today segregation is no longer enforced by the law. But separation by race continues. So does inequality.

Mavis Staples knows that the movement continues. She is still singing the music of the movement. In her 2007 CD, *We'll Never Turn Back*, she looks at homes destroyed by Hurricane Katrina. She sees that they have not been rebuilt. Looking at Mississippi schools for black children, she exclaims, "It's the 21st Century—it feels like it's 1960!"

Staples says in the liner notes:

Here it is, 2007, and there are still so many problems and social injustices in the world. . . . With this record, I hope to get across the same feeling, the same spirit and the same message as we did then—and to hopefully continue to make positive changes. Things are better but we're not where we need to be and we'll never turn back.

Black poverty rates remain high. In 2006, almost one in four black people lived in poverty. Fewer than one in 10 white people lived in poverty. The median income for a black person was only 61 percent of white median income.

Black people know that they still face discrimination. They see discrimination in hiring, in housing, and even in shopping. Most white people do not see this. Most white people think that discrimination has ended. Because they do not experience discrimination, it is invisible to them.

No laws keep black people from living in "white neighborhoods." Housing discrimination is against the law. Still, many neighborhoods are not welcoming. Some landlords still refuse to rent to black people.

In 2006, Velvie Green was named president of Glendale Community College in Arizona. She moved from Michigan to Arizona. She found an apartment to rent. Her real estate agent contacted the landlord's agent. The landlord said that he would not rent to black people. His real estate agent told Green's agent that he would not rent to black people. Velvie Green took them to court. The court said they were breaking the law. The landlord and the real estate agent were ordered to change their policies. They also had to go to classes about fair housing laws.

This is just one example of housing discrimination. Other cases happen every day. Many people do not go to court. Some feel it won't do any good. Others may not have the time and resources to follow through with a complaint.

But the civil rights movement made a huge difference. Today housing discrimination is illegal. The federal Fair Housing Act outlaws discrimination in housing. It applies to many (but not all) homes and apartments. Many states also have their own fair housing laws. The federal law applies to both selling and renting. The Fair Housing Act makes it illegal to discriminate on the basis of race, color, religion, sex, familial status, handicap, or national origin.

Today people can challenge discrimination in court. But discrimination still exists. Today's movement continues to fight against it.

## School Segregation: Then and Now

Remember Barbara Johns, the teenager who organized a school strike in 1951? Her protest against the segregated schools in Prince Edward County, Virginia, ended up in the Supreme Court. The court ordered an end to school segregation. That was a battle won.

Then the delaying tactics began. Southern states and schools said they could not act overnight. In 1955, the court agreed that they could move with "all deliberate speed." That was all the excuse they needed. Across the South, "deliberate speed" translated to delay after delay.

Prince Edward County built a new high school for black students after the 1951 protests. They kept schools strictly segregated. More lawsuits followed. Finally, in 1959, the courts ordered desegregation—immediately.

Instead of integrating, the county closed all of its schools. For five years, there were no public schools in Prince Edward County.

A private foundation opened whites-only schools. All the white children in the county attended these schools. Some paid tuition. Most were subsidized by private foundation money. For one year (1960–61), public money paid tuition for white students in the segregated private schools.

In 1963, the federal government set up a school system in Prince Edward County. The federal schools were free to all students. Black children—and three white children—attended the free schools.

In 1964, the Supreme Court ordered Prince Edward County to reopen its public schools. Justice Hugo Black wrote: "There has been entirely too much deliberation and not enough speed in enforcing the Constitutional rights which we held 10 years ago had been denied Prince Edward Negro children."

Prince Edward County public schools reopened on September 8, 1964. About 1,500 students attended. All but eight of the students were black. Real integration came only after a new superintendent took over in 1972. By the 1990s, about 40 percent of the students were white.

In other schools, north and south, segregation is still an issue.

## Jackson, Mississippi

In Jackson, Mississippi, schools did not integrate until 1970. The White Citizens Councils opened all-white private schools to avoid integration. The last of the Council schools closed in 1985.

This does not mean that the Jackson schools are integrated. A researcher at Jackson State University explains.

> We've gone from de jure to de facto segregation. . . . [My high school] opened in 1968 as an all-white school in what was at that point a high growth area. . . . I graduated 11 years later in 1979. Then it was probably 60 percent black. Now the school is all-black.

The new segregation comes because the city is mostly black. White people moved out. They went to small towns. Today most Jackson schools are 80–100 percent black.

## McComb, Mississippi

Back in the 1960s, Jackie Byrd Martin attended segregated schools in McComb. Today, she says, McComb schools are integrated, at least by law. In practice, however, the picture looks different. The schools in McComb and in nearby South Pike are at least 80 percent black. The schools in nearby North Pike are 80 percent white. A local Christian school is virtually all white.

123

In recent years, McComb has started a community dialogue. Racial reconciliation is the main topic. McComb schools are now looking at the civil rights movement, rather than ignoring it. These may be signs of change for the future.

## Chicago

In 1966, Dr. Martin Luther King Jr. marched in Chicago. He insisted that civil rights were not just a southern problem. Today, Chicago still proves him right.

In Chicago, almost one-third of all public schools were 100 percent African American in 2006. Almost one-half of all public schools were at least 90 percent African American. High school graduation rates for African American students were low.

De jure school segregation is against the law. The civil rights movement won a huge victory. But changing the law did not end the color line dividing schools. *De facto* segregation continues. Bridging this divide is work for the future.

## We Have Come So Far

The civil rights movement swept the country in the mid–20th century. In the early 1950s, parents and students challenged school segregation. They sued to overturn the laws. In 1955, Rosa Parks refused to give up her seat on the bus in Montgomery. Black people in Montgomery showed their power in a bus boycott. In 1960, stu-

Under the water in the reflecting pool at the Civil Rights Memorial, Chicago Children's Choir members touch the names of people who were killed in the civil rights movement. Moved to song, they pledge their continuing commitment to justice. *Davin Peelle*

dents began the sit-in movement, protesting lunch counter segregation. Freedom Riders challenged bus segregation. Other protests targeted segregated libraries, beaches, and movie theaters.

Across the South, thousands of protesters went to jail. Others paid an even higher price. Beatings left Freedom Riders permanently injured. People lost their jobs and businesses. Bombs destroyed homes and churches.

Many paid the highest price. Racism and hatred took their lives. Four young girls in a Birmingham church. A boy trying to protect his mother from police attack. A minister leaving a diner. A farmer in Mississippi. The head of an NAACP chapter. A woman driving from Montgomery to Selma. Three Freedom Summer volunteers. And, in 1968, Dr. Martin Luther King Jr.

They did not die in vain. The civil rights movement won a nonviolent revolution. It forever changed the United States.

In 1954, the Supreme Court said school segregation was illegal. Two years later, it ordered an end to Montgomery's bus segregation. Then Congress passed the Civil Rights Act of 1964. The next year, the Voting Rights Act became law. Racial discrimination can never again be the law of the land.

Although the laws changed, the struggle did not end. Prejudice continues into the 21st century.

- New York, 2007: A racial slur and sketch of a lynched person were drawn on a chalkboard in a locker room used by black athletes.
- Massachusetts, 2007: A man was arrested after he shouted anti-immigrant remarks and smashed a Brazilian family's window.
- Oregon, 2007: Two Latino men were attacked by a group of 20 to 30 white teenagers who taunted and threw stones at the men.
- Texas, 2007: A Muslim family's vehicles were vandalized with messages telling them to move.

The reports go on and on. A cross is burned in the front yard of an interracial couple. A gay man is beaten. A lesbian couple receive threats at their home. A black family's home is burned. Nooses are hung from trees or rearview mirrors. Nooses appear in workplaces, schools, cars.

In 2006, the FBI reported 7,720 hate crimes. About half showed racial bias. The next-largest category was religious bias. Hate crimes based on sexual orientation were third. More than 900 of the crimes expressed hatred based on national origin. Hate crimes ranged from vandalism to murder.

Atlanta city councilman John Lewis holds the March 1965 issue of *Life* magazine in his office in Atlanta, Georgia, August 7, 1986. The cover photo shows Lewis leading the first Selma, Alabama, civil rights march with Hosea Williams. Lewis, an Alabama sharecropper's son, suffered brutal beatings and humiliating sentences in the five years preceding the Voting Rights Act. *Ric Feld, Associated Press*

Laws are necessary, but they are not enough. Laws can change what people do, but not how people think or feel. That change is part of the continuing work of the movement.

## Dealing with the Here and Now

Hollis Watkins has been working for civil rights for over 40 years. In the 1960s, he was arrested, jailed, beaten, and threatened with death. When he became active in the civil rights movement, at the age of 19, his older brothers and sisters thought he was crazy. Now, he says, they are proud of him.

Today, Hollis Watkins still works for justice with Southern Echo, a leadership development and education organization in the South. He believes that the movement is still alive.

> We were dealing with the then and the there. We still have to deal with the here and the now.
>
> I say to young people today: I can't define what your movement should look like in your community today. The concerns in every community varied. There were some issues that cut across all community lines.
>
> Today the issue of education, the issue of environment—they cut across all the lines. . . . If you look at where you are today, real close to you, your family, your community—you will find a lot of things that are not right, that need to be changed. . . . Then

you have your issues that you need to mobilize and organize around.

> It starts with one person. If you begin to overcome fear, to talk to others about your concern, you will find that others see things the way you do. And that is the beginning of building your movement where you are. . . .
>
> Many of the things that we had to deal with back then, in many areas of the country still exist. Police brutality is still very prevalent. Racism still exists. It exists in different forms. Back then, when you look at the South, the Klansmen were dressed in white, hooded robes. Today a lot are dressed in black robes, serving as judges. They are in the police departments. They are sheriffs of various counties.
>
> There are plenty of issues to go around, for all of us to have more than we can do.

Hollis Watkins still works for justice. He still believes in the power of song.

> When I'm invited to go somewhere to speak to groups of people, I get them involved in singing. I don't just do a speech. . . . If they don't know a song, I teach it. All of the songs are very easy to learn. . . . People feel a lot better having truly been a part of it.

Robert Williams is a veteran of the civil rights movement. As a black teen in Alabama, he took part in the Selma to Montgomery march. He worked in the youth

Uniting the civil rights movement of the 1960s with today, the Chicago Children's Choir marched across Selma's Edmund Pettus Bridge during Freedom Tour 2007. Joann Bland, who was one of the youngest marchers in 1965, accompanied them. *Mary C. Turck*

movement of the Montgomery Improvement Association. Looking at today's world, he also sees unfinished business. He sees a continuing need to work for equality for black people in the United States.

Williams sees other issues of justice, too. "We have a wave of immigrants from Mexico and Latin America that are running into a wall of discrimination," he says. "People are exploiting them. People are making problems between black folks and immigrants. They are trying to turn it into us versus them."

Today many immigrants agree with Robert Williams. Linda Chavez is a prominent Republican activist and businesswoman. She wrote in 2007:

Some people just don't like Mexicans—or anyone else from south of the border. They think Latinos are freeloaders and welfare cheats who are too lazy to learn English. They think Latinos have too many babies, and that Latino kids will dumb down our schools. They think Latinos are dirty, diseased, indolent and more prone to criminal behavior. They think Latinos are just too different from us ever to become real Americans.

Another prominent writer reports that today's anti-immigrant movement is the "biggest explosion of anti-Hispanic sentiment I have seen since I arrived in this country three decades ago."

Anti-immigrant groups focus on Latinos. Many denounce speaking Spanish in public. Some say that immigration threatens white people, who themselves are the descendants of immigrants. Their prejudice extends even to Latinos who are U.S. citizens.

Latinos and immigrants feel the force of prejudice. So do Muslims in the United States. In 2007, U.S. congressman Peter King said that there are "too many mosques in this country." He accused mosques of being extremist. Other political leaders said that Islam is like fascism. Some accused Islam of supporting terrorism. A 2006 poll found that more than one in five people said they would not want a Muslim as a neighbor. In the same poll, 39 percent said they felt prejudice against Muslims.

Girl at immigrant rights march in Minnesota in 2006. *Mary C. Turck*

Anti-Muslim prejudice is tied to anti-Arab prejudice. Not all Arabs are Muslims. Many Muslims are not Arabs. Not all Arabs are immigrants. U.S.-born Muslims and Arabs report being told to "go back where you came from." They report being called terrorists.

## Young People Look at Civil Rights Today

Youth in the Chicago Children's Choir are far removed from the civil rights movement of the 1950s and 1960s.

They live in a world, a country, and a city where race still matters. They see the need for continuing work for racial justice. They also see other important civil rights struggles.

Some discrimination is still legal. In 2007, U.S. law still allowed discrimination against gay and lesbian people. In 33 states, it was legal to fire a person because of his or her sexual orientation.

In the 1960s, homosexuality was an issue in the civil rights movement. Bayard Rustin was a long-time leader. Born in 1912, he was one of the elders of the movement. He helped to organize the first Freedom Rides in the 1940s. He continued to work for civil rights. He was a leader in organizing the 1963 March on Washington. He was also a homosexual.

In those days, homosexuality was illegal and a matter of deep shame to many people. When Rustin's homosexuality became publicly known, other movement leaders decided that they could not afford to associate with him. They insisted that he could not have any public part in the march.

Women's rights were also an issue. At the March on Washington, women were excluded. Only the male leaders marched in front. Years later, Coretta Scott King wrote about how unjust this felt. She and other wives had shared the dangers of the movement. Now they were excluded.

Beanie Meadow graduated from high school and the Chicago Children's Choir in 2007. She believes that work for civil rights is still needed.

"When I was in the neighborhood choir we toured in Georgia and we performed for audiences that were all white or all black—they were not integrated, even today. Our hope is that, when they see us performing, they can see that black and white people together are singing 'black' songs and 'white' songs, and they'll see that we can all make music together and there's no real difference. Of course, there is cultural difference, but that is to be celebrated, not used to separate us.

"I believe in affirmative action. There are still people who are racist. There are prejudices in society that I have not been able to avoid. Even I—when I'm walking down the street at night in Hyde Park, get more nervous when I see a black person than a white person. It's like ingrained in me, and I hope my children won't have that ingrained in them."

**"Our hope is that, when they see us performing . . . they'll see that we can all make music together and there's no real difference."**

Lily Espinoza spent 10 years in the Chicago Children's Choir, graduating in 2007. "Our world still does not accept African Americans as equals," she says. "We know that. We are rife with prejudice in this country. As far as civil rights currently, gay civil rights [are still an issue]. Gay marriage is something that I'm really adamant about—it's ridiculous that it is still being debated."

Another 2007 choir graduate, Kyle Sircus, agrees. "We've overcome a lot, but there is a lot of hidden racism that has expanded to be not just white versus African American, but international racism, too. Beyond that issue, a lot has to do with our own civil rights as Americans, civil liberties that are being denied—the issue of gay marriage and tons of different stuff."

**"We've overcome a lot, but there is a lot of hidden racism . . ."**

In 1964, opponents of civil rights supported adding protection for women to civil rights bills. They thought that giving women equal rights was a ridiculous idea. They hoped that adding this to the bill would mean a sure defeat for civil rights. Instead, the 1964 Civil Rights Act passed. It guaranteed equal rights for all races—and for women, too.

# Music in the Movement Today

Two examples show the continuing role of music in movements for justice. The first is the musical response to Hurricane Katrina, and the second is One Voice Mixed Chorus.

## Katrina in New Orleans

Hurricane Katrina hit the Gulf Coast in 2005, destroying large parts of New Orleans and towns in Mississippi. Before the hurricane, two-thirds of New Orleans residents were black. The neighborhoods hit hardest by the hurricane were poor and black. The federal government was not quick to respond to the disaster. Many people saw racism in the slow and inadequate response.

By 2008, business and tourist sections of the city had been rebuilt. The city's poor neighborhoods had not. Hundreds of thousands of families lost their homes. Fewer than half were able to return.

New Orleans is a historic home of music and jazz. Musicians around the world responded to the disaster. Some organized benefit concerts. Stevie Wonder recorded "Shelter in the Rain" and donated all proceeds to Katrina relief. Other musicians wrote protest songs about Katrina. Prince recorded "S.S.T.," which focused on Katrina. He sang:

*Did u have open arms 4 each and everybody U met*
*Or did U let them die in the rain? Endless war, Poverty or*
   *hurricane . . .*

The Chicago Children's Choir visited New Orleans on the Freedom Tour. They spent a day working on a rebuilding project, and sang for victims of Katrina. They also saw how Hurricane Katrina put a spotlight on the racial divisions that still plague the country.

## One Voice in Minnesota

"Building community and creating social change by raising our voices in song." One Voice Mixed Chorus proclaims this mission on its Web page (www.ovmc.org). One Voice unites gay, lesbian, bisexual, and transgendered people and their straight allies. The chorus is committed to both musical excellence and outreach. Its repertoire ranges from classical to contemporary music, and includes freedom songs.

One Voice Mixed Chorus in concert. *Courtesy of One Voice*

One Voice has met with *homophobia*—prejudice against lesbian, gay, bisexual, and transgendered people. One rural school canceled its concert. In another community, parents kept children home from school so they could not see or hear One Voice.

Other people have driven three or four hours to attend One Voice concerts. One chorus member says: "I think the sense of isolation and confusion is greatly lessened by even knowing groups such as One Voice Mixed Chorus exist."

The civil rights movement is not over. As long as prejudice continues, the movement has work to do. That work might be lawsuits, marches, demonstrations, or education. So long as people stand up for justice, the movement continues. The drumbeat for justice continues. The words change, but the melody of the movement goes on.

If you would like to learn more about civil rights and the music of the movement, this list of resources will give you places to begin.

## Web Sites

**The official City of McComb Web site**
www.mccomb-ms.com
**The unofficial McComb city Web site**
www.mccombms.com
**McComb Legacies**
www.mccomblegacies.org
*As of this writing, the first two Web sites made no mention of the civil rights movement. They did not link to the McComb Legacies site. The McComb Legacies Web site did link to both of the others. McComb Legacies provided a rich history of the civil rights movement in McComb.*

**Urban League**
www.nul.org
*The official Urban League Web site provides information on the league's activities today.*

**Congress of Racial Equality**
www.core-online.org
*The official CORE Web site provides information on CORE's activities today.*

**National Association for the Advancement of Colored People**
www.naacp.org
*The official NAACP Web site provides information on the NAACP's activities today.*

**CRM Vets Web site**
www.crmvet.org
*The Civil Rights Movement Veterans provide stories, oral history, photographs, poetry, discussions, and more.*

**Chicago Children's Choir**
www.ccchoir.org
*The CCC Web site includes songs and stories as well as the CCC schedule and lists of CDs.*

**The Highlander Center**
www.highlandercenter.org

*Highlander Center work and educational programs continue today, with photos covering over 70 years.*

### National Civil Rights Museum
www.civilrightsmuseum.org
*The museum traces civil rights history through its Web site as well as in person.*

### Southern Poverty Law Center
www.splcenter.org
*The Southern Poverty Law Center continues to work against prejudice and hate crimes. Its Web site includes links to educational materials as well as current news.*

### Eyes on the Prize
www.pbs.org/wgbh/amex/eyesontheprize
*This PBS series provides a history of the civil rights movement.*

### The Long Walk of Nelson Mandela
www.pbs.org/wgbh/pages/frontline/shows/mandela
*Nelson Mandela and South African history come alive in this documentary.*

## Music

Today you can use the Internet to find music from any of the artists mentioned in this book. A few excellent historical collections of civil rights movement music are listed below.

### *All for Freedom*
Sweet Honey in the Rock (Music for Little People, 1989).

*Freedom songs recorded for children by Sweet Honey in the Rock, whose roots lie deep in the civil rights movement.*

### *The Best of Ladysmith Black Mambazo*
Ladysmith Black Mambazo (Shanachie, 1992).
*The foremost South African singing group is the best choice to introduce South African music.*

### *The Long Road to Freedom: An Anthology of Black Music*
Various artists (Buddha, 2001).
*This five-CD set is accompanied by a 140-page book—an incredible resource for serious musicians and historians.*

### *Mahalia Jackson: Gospels, Spirituals and Hymns*
Mahalia Jackson (Sony, 1991, 1998).
*A comprehensive collection of gospel music by the Queen of Gospel.*

### *Sing for Freedom: Civil Rights Movement Songs*
Various artists (Smithsonian Folkways, 1990).
*Features 26 songs and speeches from the civil rights movement, recorded during the 1960s.*

### *Voices of The Civil Rights Movement: Black American Freedom Songs 1960–1966*
Various artists (Smithsonian Folkways, 1997).
*The two-CD, 43-song compilation was recorded live in mass meetings in churches between 1960 and 1966 by singers including the SNCC Freedom Singers.*

### *We'll Never Turn Back*
Mavis Staples (ANTI, 2007).

Mavis Staples brings the music of the movement into the 21st century, including meditations on Katrina in New Orleans and poverty today.

## Videos/DVDs

### Freedom Song
Directed by Phil Alden Robinson, starring Danny Glover (Turner Home Entertainment, 2006).
*This movie tells a story of the civil rights movement through the eyes of a black teenager in a small Mississippi town. The story of ordinary people living in extraordinary times, made with passion and eloquence, and with the guidance of former SNCC president Chuck McDew.*

### Four Little Girls
Directed by Spike Lee (HBO Home Video, 2001).
*This documentary, produced by Spike Lee, focuses on the civil rights movement in Birmingham and the events leading up to the 1963 church bombing.*

### Gentleman's Agreement
Directed by Elia Kazan, starring Gregory Peck (20th Century Fox, 1947).
### Guess Who's Coming to Dinner
Directed by Stanley Kramer, starring Sidney Poitier, Katherine Hepburn, Spencer Tracy (Sony Pictures, 1967).
*These are two older movies about prejudice. The "gentleman's agreement" discriminates against Jews, and the surprise dinner guest is the African American fiancé of a white woman, coming to meet her parents and face their prejudices.*

### Hoop Dreams
Directed by Steve James (Criterion, 1994).
*This is a documentary record of the lives of two young African American men from Chicago's inner city. Each of them hopes that basketball will be a ticket out of poverty. The obstacles they face include the manipulation of their hopes and talents by college and professional basketball systems.*

### A Dry, White Season
Directed by Euzhan Palcy, starring Donald Sutherland and Marlon Brando (MGM, 1989).
*This movie shows the recent history of apartheid in South Africa through the eyes of a white schoolteacher during the Soweto uprising.*

### Mississippi Burning
Directed by Alan Parker (MGM, 1988).
*This movie has been criticized for showing the FBI in an overly flattering light. While the criticism is accurate, the movie is valuable for its true stories of the murder of three young civil rights workers, the burning of churches, and the violent opposition to the civil rights movement in Mississippi in the 1960s.*

### Roots
Directed by Marvin J. Chomsky (Warner Home Video, 1977).
*This miniseries is based on a book by Alex Haley that traces his own family roots from the 20th-century United States back to Africa. The richness of African culture, the cruelty of slavery, and the strength of African American families are evident in this powerful drama. When Roots was broadcast as a television series in 1987, it drew wide audiences and inspired a surge of interest in family histories among people of all ethnic backgrounds.*

## Books

Bridges, Ruby. *Through My Eyes*. New York: Scholastic, 1999.

Clark, Septima, with Cynthia Stokes Brown. *Ready from Within: A First Person Narrative*. Lawrenceville, NJ: Africa World Press, 1990.

Colman, Penny. *Fannie Lou Hamer and the Fight for the Vote*. Minneapolis: Millbrook Press, 1994.

Curtis, Christopher Paul. *The Watsons Go to Birmingham—1963*. New York: Random House, 1997.

Evers-Williams, Myrlie, with Melinda Blue. *Watch Me Fly*. New York: Little, Brown, 1999.

Levine, Ellen. *Freedom's Children: Young Civil Rights Activists Tell Their Own Stories*. New York: Penguin Young Readers Group, 2000.

Parks, Rosa, with Jim Haskins. *Rosa Parks: My Story*. New York: Dial Books, 1992.

Rappaport, Doreen. *Nobody Gonna Turn Me 'Round: Stories and Songs of the Civil Rights Movement*. Cambridge, MA: Candlewick Press, 2006.

Turck, Mary C. *The Civil Rights Movement for Kids*. Chicago: Chicago Review Press, 2000.

This appendix contains words to some songs of the civil rights movement that you may want to sing. Most of them are traditional songs, and you should feel free to change the words—as others have before you.

## Ain't Gonna Let Nobody Turn Me Around
(Traditional)

Ain't gonna let nobody turn me around
Turn me around, turn me around
Ain't gonna let nobody turn me around
Gonna keep on a'walkin, keep on a'talkin
Gonna build a brand new world.

Ain't gonna let segregation turn me around . . .
Ain't gonna let discrimination turn me around . . .
Ain't gonna let no politicians turn me around . . .

## The Battle of Jericho
See p. 51

## Down by the Riverside
(Traditional)

I'm gonna lay down my heavy load
Down by the riverside
Down by the riverside
Down by the riverside
I'm gonna lay down my heavy load
Down by the riverside
Gonna study war no more.

Chorus:
I ain't gonna study war no more
I ain't gonna study war no more
I ain't gonna study war no more
I ain't gonna study war no more.

I'm gonna lay down my sword and shield
Down by the riverside
Down by the riverside
Down by the riverside
I'm gonna lay down my sword and shield

*Down by the riverside*
*Gonna study war no more.*

Chorus

*I'm gonna put on my long white robe*
*Down by the riverside*
*Down by the riverside*
*Down by the riverside*
*I'm gonna put on my long white robe*
*Down by the riverside*
*Gonna study war no more.*

Chorus

**The Freedom Song**
See p. 79

**He's Got the Whole World in His Hands**
(Traditional)

*He's got the whole world, in his hands*
*He's got the whole world, in his hands*
*He's got the whole world, in his hands*
*He's got the whole world, in his hands*

*He's got the tiny little baby, in his hands*
*He's got the tiny little baby, in his hands*
*He's got the tiny little baby, in his hands*
*He's got the whole world, in his hands*

Other verses:
*He's got you and me, brother, in his hands . . .*
*He's got you and me, sister, in his hands . . .*
*He's got everybody here, in his hands . . .*

**If You Miss Me from the Back of the Bus**
See p. 52

**Kum Ba Ya, My Lord**
(Traditional)

*Kum ba ya, my Lord, kum ba ya*
*Kum ba ya, my Lord, kum ba ya*
*Kum ba ya, my Lord, kum ba ya*
*Oh, Lord, Kum ba ya*

*Someone's crying, Lord, kum ba ya*
*Someone's crying, Lord, kum ba ya*
*Someone's crying, Lord, kum ba ya*
*Oh, Lord, Kum ba ya*

Other verses:
*Someone's praying, Lord . . .*
*Someone's hoping, Lord . . .*
*Someone's singing, Lord . . .*

**Lift Every Voice and Sing**
See p. 29

**Run Children Run**
See p. 18

**Swing Low, Sweet Chariot**
(Traditional)

*Swing low, sweet chariot coming for to carry me home*
*Swing low, sweet chariot coming for to carry me home*

*I looked over Jordan and what did I see*
*Coming for to carry me home*
*A band of angels is coming after me*
*Coming for to carry me home.*

*Swing low, sweet chariot coming for to carry me home*
*Swing low, sweet chariot coming for to carry me home*

*If you come to heaven before I do*
*Coming for to carry me home*
*Tell all my friends I'll be coming there, too*
*Coming for to carry me home.*

*Swing low, sweet chariot coming for to carry me home*
*Swing low, sweet chariot coming for to carry me home*

**This Land Is Your Land**
See p. 93

**This Little Light of Mine**
(Traditional)

*This little light of mine, I'm going to let it shine*
*This little light of mine, I'm going to let it shine*
*This little light of mine, I'm going to let it shine*

*Let it shine, let it shine, let it shine*

*Everywhere I go, I'm going to let it shine*
*Everywhere I go, I'm going to let it shine*
*Everywhere I go, I'm going to let it shine*
*Let it shine, let it shine, let it shine*

*All in my home, I'm going to let it shine . . .*
*All around this city . . .*
*When the night is dark . . .*

**Wade in the Water**
See p. 19

**We Shall Overcome**

*We shall overcome*
*We shall overcome*
*We shall overcome some day*
*Deep in my heart, I do believe*
*We shall overcome some day.*

*Black and white together*
*Black and white together*
*Black and white together*
*Deep in my heart, I do believe*
*We shall overcome some day.*

*We shall live in peace*
*We shall live in peace*
*We shall live in peace*

*Deep in my heart, I do believe*
*We shall overcome some day.*

**We Shall Not Be Moved**
(Traditional)

*We shall not*
*We shall not be moved*
*We shall not be moved*
*Just like a tree that's planted by the water*
*We shall not be moved.*

*Black and white together*
*We shall not be moved*
*Black and white together*
*We shall not be moved*
*Black and white together*
*We shall not be moved*
*Just like a tree that's planted by the water*
*We shall not be moved.*

**When the Saints Go Marching In**
(Traditional)

*Oh, when the saints go marching in*
*Oh, when the saints go marching in*
*Oh, Lord, I want to be in that number*
*When the saints go marching in*

*And when the sun begins to shine*
*And when the sun begins to shine*
*Oh, Lord, I want to be in that number*
*When the sun begins to shine*

*Oh, when the saints go marching in*
*Oh, when the saints go marching in*
*Oh, Lord, I want to be in that number*
*When the saints go marching in*

Other verses:
*Oh, when we march around the throne . . .*
*Oh, when the time shall be no more . . .*

# Songs on the Road to Freedom CD

## A Message from the Chicago Children's Choir

*"I have been deeply concerned about this country and the world in which we live. My way of attempting to help change it has been working with children and youth in and through music to assist them to a deeper understanding of the whole process of building and maintaining a culture that nourishes and ministers to people."*

—Reverend Christopher Moore (1929–1987),
founder of Chicago Children's Choir

The 2006/2007 year marked the 50th anniversary of the Chicago Children's Choir, encouraging us to reflect more deeply upon our founding principles. What began as the dynamic and enduring vision of Reverend Christopher Moore—to bring together children from diverse backgrounds to learn about themselves, others, and the world around them—is now the largest choral music education organization in the country, serving nearly 3,000 children each year, with over 75 percent from low-income households.

As this milestone year came to an end, singers from our Concert Choir, reflecting the racial, ethnic, and socioeconomic diversity of Chicago, embarked on a Freedom Tour of the southern United States. Included were performances in Birmingham, Montgomery, Selma, and Memphis, as well as concerts for victims of Hurricane Katrina in Waveland, Mississippi, and New Orleans. This recording features music performed throughout the tour.

With these songs, we honor our roots in the civil rights movement as well as the people who faced the incomprehensible struggles firsthand. Much of the music comes directly from that time, such as "Precious Lord," "Birmingham Sunday," and "Strange Fruit," while others were written in the past few years. We also sing the antiapartheid music of South Africa, where people similarly struggled for freedom and justice.

It is important for our young singers and those they touch to understand our country's struggle for civil rights and apply those lessons to solving current social tensions and injustices for all people. Our belief is that this understanding will help Reverend Moore's dream of a peacefully integrated society become a reality.

We are grateful to the McCormick Tribune Foundation for making this recording and the Freedom Tour possible, as well as to the singers of Chicago Children's Choir who keep the dream alive!

Josephine Lee<br>
Artistic Director<br>
Chicago Children's Choir

1. Ain't Gonna Let Nobody Turn Me 'Round (Civil Rights Movement Song, arr. Mollie Stone)
*We're gonna keep on a-walkin', keep on a-talkin', marchin' up to freedom land.*

2. MLK (U2, arr. Bib Chilcott) Soloist: Phillip Armstrong
*"In Memphis, at the site of Dr. Martin Luther King Jr.'s assassination, there is a monument with these words from Genesis 37:19–20: 'They said one to another, behold, here cometh the dreamer . . . Let us slay him . . . and we shall see what will become of his dreams.' While singing at the site, hearing the hauntingly beautiful words of 'MLK' floating from their voices, there was comfort in knowing that in these children his dreams have been realized." —Judy Hanson, Director of Choral Programs*

3. The Battle of Jericho (Traditional Spiritual, arr. Moses Hogan) Soloist: Jasmine Henderson

*Just as Joshua broke down the walls of Jericho, the Chicago Children's Choir works to break down walls that divide people, whether racial, ethnic, or socioeconomic.*

4. Precious Lord (Thomas A. Dorsey)
*Singing one of Dr. King's favorite hymns of comfort and rejuvenation is a constant reminder of the strength he had and where he found that strength.*

5. Birmingham Sunday (Richard Farina, arr. Ted Hearne)
*"In 1963, a bomb deliberately placed near the basement of the 16th Street Baptist Church in Birmingham exploded, killing four African American girls. Performing this song, especially in the church where the tragedy struck, reminds us how critical it is that we all keep 'singing of freedom.'" —John Goodwin, Principal Accompanist and Conductor in Residence*

6. Murder on the Road in Alabama (Len H. Chandler Jr., arr. Ted Hearne) Soloists: Jasmine Henderson, Timothy Fett, and Phillip Armstrong
*Viola Liuzzo, a white nurse from Detroit, had seen Bloody Sunday on television. Two weeks later, she and thousands like her were marching with Dr. King from Selma to Montgomery. Afterward, as she was shuttling people to the airport, a car full of Klansmen caught up with her on Route 80. They fired two shots through her car window, killing her instantly. Len Chandler, a classically trained musician turned folk singer/songwriter who had also marched, drove past the murder scene, and was inspired to write this song using Mrs. Liuzzo's death as a metaphor for all of the hatred and sorrow in America at that time.*

7. Run Children Run (Traditional Field Yell, arr. Stephen Hatfield) Soloists: Mitchell Owens, Adriana Flocco, Timothy Fett, Jasmine Henderson, Kyle Sircus, and Dana Buetow
*I got a right, you got a right, we got a right to the tree of life.*

8. Freedom Train (Rollo Dilworth) Commissioned by Chicago Children's Choir and Josephine Lee in honor of the 50th anniversary of the Chicago Children's Choir
*This was the perfect song to open all of our concerts on the Freedom Tour, quoting melodies from past spirituals in an energetic setting sung by youth— looking to the past to inspire the future.*

9. When Love Wins the Day (Music by Roger Treece/Lyrics by Don Rosler) Commissioned by Chicago Children's Choir and Josephine Lee in 2005
*"Whether it's a quest for a simple drink of water at a 'whites only' fountain or one's desire to unroll a dream, passing a torch of truth any distance always involves dissonance, harmony, struggle, exhilaration and a voice as powerful as Dr. King's to help lead the way." —Don Rosler, Lyricist*

10. Strange Fruit (Abel Meeropol a.k.a. Lewis Allen, arr. Kristina Boerger)
*"To prevent such horrors from happening again, we must speak honestly about our history. Every time the singers perform 'Strange Fruit,' they delve deeper into its haunting poetry, feeling a stronger connection to what happened in the past, and a determination to speak out against prejudice and violence in the future." —Mollie Stone, Chicago Children's Choir alumna and Associate Conductor*

11. Ballad of Harry T. Moore (arr. Bernice Johnson Reagon) Soloists: Lauryn Payne, Cathy Ludwig, Lakeyah Scales, Corean Reynolds, Jasmine Henderson, Theresa Reyes, Nora Richards, Taylor Varndell, Lauren Robinson, and Adriana Flocco
*This folk song is an adaptation of a 1952 Langston Hughes poem about the death of a Florida civil rights organizer.*

12. We Need a Word (W. Mitchell Owens III, Chicago Children's Choir class of 2009) Commissioned by Chicago Children's Choir and Josephine Lee in honor of the 50th anniversary of the Chicago Children's Choir
*"Inspired by eight years in Chicago Children's Choir, a young singer wrote this song based on his life experience and Dr. King's universal message of love and understanding. We cannot ignore that we all need a word for whoever/whatever is the guiding force in each of our lives at this time." —Josephine Lee, Artistic Director*

13. Nkosi Somandla (South African Xhosa Song) Soloist: Phillip Armstrong
*Translation: "Lord our God, dry the tears of your children." The antiapartheid movement in South Africa was inspired by the methodology of the American civil rights movement against racially institutionalized inequality and injustice. As such, music played an important role in both struggles for freedom, often using similar imagery.*

14. Iindonga zaJericho (South African Zulu Song)
*Translation: "We are taking down the walls of Jericho, they*

*fall!" Although the song comes from the biblical story of Joshua and the Battle of Jericho, it is actually used as a metaphor for the struggle against apartheid. "The walls" in this case are the walls of the apartheid government.*

15. Shosholoza (South African Antiapartheid Song)
*Translation: "The train of freedom comes from the mountain. Stimela pushes the train to South Africa."*

16. A Prayin' Spirit (Twinkie Clark)
*For centuries, spirituals have evoked positive messages of hope and salvation to uplift those struggling for freedom and equality.*

17. We Shall Overcome (Traditional) Soloist: Phillip Armstrong
*The power of this civil rights movement anthem continues to inspire hope throughout the world for a peacefully integrated society.*

18. Ain't Gonna Let Nobody Turn Me 'Round (reprise)

More information and a full list of credits for *Songs on the Road to Freedom* are available on the CCC Web site at www.ccchoir.org/choir-store/freedom-song.